2018 SQA Past Papers & Hodder Gibson Model Paper with Answers

Advanced Higher
MATHEMATICS

Model Paper,
2016, 2017 & 2018 Exams

HODDER
GIBSON
AN HACHETTE UK COMPANY

This book contains the official 2016, 2017 and 2018 Exams for Advanced Higher Maths, with associated SQA-approved answers modified from the official marking instructions that accompany the paper.

In addition the book contains a model paper, together with answers, plus study skills advice. This paper, which may include a limited number of previously published SQA questions, has been specially commissioned by Hodder Gibson, and has been written by experienced senior teachers and examiners in line with the Advanced Higher syllabus and assessment outlines. This is not SQA material but has been devised to provide further practice for Advanced Higher examinations.

Hachette UK's policy is to use papers that are natural, renewable and recyclable products and made from wood grown in sustainable forests. The logging and manufacturing processes are expected to conform to the environmental regulations of the country of origin.

Orders: please contact Bookpoint Ltd, 130 Park Drive, Milton Park, Abingdon, Oxon OX14 4SE. Telephone: (44) 01235 827827. Fax: (44) 01235 400454. Lines are open 9.00–5.00, Monday to Saturday, with a 24-hour message answering service. Visit our website at www.hoddereducation.co.uk. Hodder Gibson can also be contacted directly at hoddergibson@hodder.co.uk

This collection first published in 2018 by
Hodder Gibson, an imprint of Hodder Education,
An Hachette UK Company
211 St Vincent Street
Glasgow G2 5QY

Typeset by Aptara, Inc.

Printed in the UK

A catalogue record for this title is available from the British Library

ISBN: 978-1-5104-5488-0

2 1

2019 2018

MIX
Paper from
responsible sources
FSC™ C104740

Introduction

Advanced Higher Mathematics

The course

The Advanced Higher Mathematics course is designed to build upon and extend the skills, knowledge and understanding that you have attained in the Higher Mathematics course (or equivalent qualification). It enables you to develop further skills in calculus, algebra and geometry. Areas such as number theory, complex numbers and matrices are introduced as well as processes of rigorous proof.

How the course is assessed

To gain the course award, you must pass the three Units:
- Methods in Algebra and Calculus
- Applications of Algebra and Calculus
- Geometry, Proof and Systems of Equations

as well as the examination.

The Units are assessed internally on a pass/fail basis.

The examination is set and marked by experienced practitioners appointed by SQA.

The course award is graded A–D, the grade being determined by the total mark you score in the examination.

The examination

The examination is a three-hour paper with a total of 100 marks, in which the use of a calculator is permitted. A formulae list will be provided (see page two of the 2018 exam).

The question paper consists of short- and extended-response questions that require the application of skills developed in the course. You are expected to communicate responses clearly and to justify solutions.

Further details can be found in the Advanced Higher Mathematics section on the SQA website: www.sqa.org.uk/sqa/48507.html.

Key tips for your success

Practise! Practise! Practise!

DOING maths questions is the most effective use of your study time. You will benefit much more from spending 30 minutes doing maths questions than spending several hours copying out notes or reading a maths textbook. Practise basic skills such as the product and quotient rules regularly.

Prior learning

Ensure that you know trigonometric identities and other relevant formulae from the Higher Mathematics course, as well as essential basic techniques such as solving quadratic equations.

Show all working clearly

The instructions on the front of the exam paper state that "Full credit will be given only to solutions which contain appropriate working." A "correct" answer with no working may only be awarded partial marks or even no marks at all. An incomplete answer will be awarded marks for any appropriate working.

Attempt every question, even if you are not sure whether you are correct or not. Your solution may contain working which will gain some marks. A blank response is certain to be awarded no marks.

Never cross out working unless you have something better to replace it with.

Ensure that you communicate reasons for what you have done, wherever appropriate. In particular, in proof and "show that" questions, include all lines of working.

Marking instructions

Ensure that you look at the detailed marking instructions of model papers and past papers. They provide further advice and guidelines as well as showing you precisely where, and for what, marks are awarded.

Extended-response questions

You should look for connections between parts of questions, particularly where there are three or four sections to a question. These are almost always linked and, in some instances, an earlier result in part (a) or (b) is needed and its use would avoid further repeated work.

Accuracy

Where possible, use exact values; decimal approximations may lead to inaccuracies which could cost you marks.

Notation

In all questions, make sure that you use the correct notation. In particular, for integration questions, remember to include "dx" within your integral. When finding an indefinite integral, remember to include the constant of integration in your answer.

Radians

Remember to work in radians when attempting any question involving both trigonometry and calculus.

Simplify

Get into the habit of simplifying expressions before doing any further work with them. This should make all subsequent work easier.

Good luck!

Remember that the rewards for passing Advanced Higher Mathematics are well worth it! Your pass will help you get the future you want for yourself. In the exam, be confident in your own ability; if you're not sure how to answer a question, trust your instincts and give it a go anyway – keep calm and don't panic! GOOD LUCK!

Study Skills – what you need to know to pass exams!

General exam revision: 20 top tips

When preparing for exams, it is easy to feel unsure of where to start or how to revise. This guide to general exam revision provides a good starting place, and, as these are very general tips, they can be applied to all your exams.

1. Start revising in good time.

Don't leave revision until the last minute – this will make you panic and it will be difficult to learn. Make a revision timetable that counts down the weeks to go.

2. Work to a study plan.

Set up sessions of work spread through the weeks ahead. Make sure each session has a focus and a clear purpose. What will you study, when and why? Be realistic about what you can achieve in each session, and don't be afraid to adjust your plans as needed.

3. Make sure you know exactly when your exams are.

Get your exam dates from the SQA website and use the timetable builder tool to create your own exam schedule. You will also get a personalised timetable from your school, but this might not be until close to the exam period.

4. Make sure that you know the topics that make up each course.

Studying is easier if material is in manageable chunks – why not use the SQA topic headings or create your own from your class notes? Ask your teacher for help on this if you are not sure.

5. Break the chunks up into even smaller bits.

The small chunks should be easier to cope with. Remember that they fit together to make larger ideas. Even the process of chunking down will help!

6. Ask yourself these key questions for each course:

- Are all topics compulsory or are there choices?
- Which topics seem to come up time and time again?
- Which topics are your strongest and which are your weakest?

Use your answers to these questions to work out how much time you will need to spend revising each topic.

7. Make sure you know what to expect in the exam.

The subject-specific introduction to this book will help with this. Make sure you can answer these questions:

- How is the paper structured?
- How much time is there for each part of the exam?
- What types of question are involved? These will vary depending on the subject so read the subject-specific section carefully.

8. Past papers are a vital *revision tool!*

Use past papers to support your revision wherever possible. This book contains the answers and mark schemes too – refer to these carefully when checking your work. Using the mark scheme is useful; even if you don't manage to get all the marks available first time when you first practise, it helps you identify how to extend and develop your answers to get more marks next time – and of course, in the real exam.

9. Use study methods that work well for you.

People study and learn in different ways. Reading and looking at diagrams suits some students. Others prefer to listen and hear material – what about reading out loud or getting a friend or family member to do this for you? You could also record and play back material.

10. There are three tried and tested ways to make material stick in your long-term memory:

- Practising – e.g. rehearsal, repeating
- Organising – e.g. making drawings, lists, diagrams, tables, memory aids
- Elaborating – e.g. incorporating the material into a story or an imagined journey

11. Learn actively.

Most people prefer to learn actively – for example, making notes, highlighting, redrawing and redrafting, making up memory aids, or writing past paper answers. A good way to stay engaged and inspired is to mix and match these methods – find the combination that best suits you. This is likely to vary depending on the topic or subject.

12. Be an expert.

Be sure to have a few areas in which you feel you are an expert. This often works because at least some of them will come up, which can boost confidence.

13. Try some visual methods.

Use symbols, diagrams, charts, flashcards, post-it notes etc. Don't forget – the brain takes in chunked images more easily than loads of text.

14. Remember – practice makes perfect.

Work on difficult areas again and again. Look and read – then test yourself. You cannot do this too much.

15. Try past papers against the clock.

Practise writing answers in a set time. This is a good habit from the start but is especially important when you get closer to exam time.

16. Collaborate with friends.

Test each other and talk about the material – this can really help. Two brains are better than one! It is amazing how talking about a problem can help you solve it.

17. Know your weaknesses.

Ask your teacher for help to identify what you don't know. Try to do this as early as possible. If you are having trouble, it is probably with a difficult topic, so your teacher will already be aware of this – most students will find it tough.

18. Have your materials organised and ready.

Know what is needed for each exam:

- Do you need a calculator or a ruler?
- Should you have pencils as well as pens?
- Will you need water or paper tissues?

19. Make full use of school resources.

Find out what support is on offer:

- Are there study classes available?
- When is the library open?
- When is the best time to ask for extra help?
- Can you borrow textbooks, study guides, past papers, etc.?
- Is school open for Easter revision?

20. Keep fit and healthy!

Try to stick to a routine as much as possible, including with sleep. If you are tired, sluggish or dehydrated, it is difficult to see how concentration is even possible. Combine study with relaxation, drink plenty of water, eat sensibly, and get fresh air and exercise – all these things will help more than you could imagine. Good luck!

ADVANCED HIGHER

Model Paper

Whilst this Model Paper has been specially commissioned by Hodder Gibson for use as practice for the Advanced Higher (for Curriculum for Excellence) exams, the key reference documents remain the SQA Past Papers 2016, 2017 and 2018.

National
Qualifications
MODEL PAPER

Mathematics

Duration — 3 hours

Total marks — 100

Attempt ALL questions.

You may use a calculator.

Full credit will be given only to solutions which contain appropriate working.

State the units for your answer where appropriate.

Write your answers clearly in the answer booklet provided. In the answer booklet, you must clearly identify the question number you are attempting.

Use **blue** or **black** ink.

Before leaving the examination room you must give your answer booklet to the Invigilator; if you do not, you may lose all the marks for this paper.

FORMULAE LIST

Standard derivatives	
$f(x)$	$f'(x)$
$\sin^{-1} x$	$\dfrac{1}{\sqrt{1-x^2}}$
$\cos^{-1} x$	$-\dfrac{1}{\sqrt{1-x^2}}$
$\tan^{-1} x$	$\dfrac{1}{1+x^2}$
$\tan x$	$\sec^2 x$
$\cot x$	$-\operatorname{cosec}^2 x$
$\sec x$	$\sec x \tan x$
$\operatorname{cosec} x$	$-\operatorname{cosec} x \cot x$
$\ln x$	$\dfrac{1}{x}$
e^x	e^x

Standard integrals	
$f(x)$	$\int f(x)\,dx$
$\sec^2(ax)$	$\dfrac{1}{a}\tan(ax)+c$
$\dfrac{1}{\sqrt{a^2-x^2}}$	$\sin^{-1}\left(\dfrac{x}{a}\right)+c$
$\dfrac{1}{a^2+x^2}$	$\dfrac{1}{a}\tan^{-1}\left(\dfrac{x}{a}\right)+c$
$\dfrac{1}{x}$	$\ln|x|+c$
e^{ax}	$\dfrac{1}{a}e^{ax}+c$

Summations

(Arithmetic series) $\qquad S_n = \dfrac{1}{2}n[2a+(n-1)d]$

(Geometric series) $\qquad S_n = \dfrac{a(1-r^n)}{1-r}, r \neq 1$

$$\sum_{r=1}^{n} r = \frac{n(n+1)}{2}, \quad \sum_{r=1}^{n} r^2 = \frac{n(n+1)(2n+1)}{6}, \quad \sum_{r=1}^{n} r^3 = \frac{n^2(n+1)^2}{4}$$

Binomial theorem

$$(a+b)^n = \sum_{r=0}^{n} \binom{n}{r} a^{n-r} b^r \text{ where } \binom{n}{r} = {}^nC_r = \frac{n!}{r!(n-r)!}$$

Maclaurin expansion

$$f(x) = f(0) + f'(0)x + \frac{f''(0)x^2}{2!} + \frac{f'''(0)x^3}{3!} + \frac{f^{iv}(0)x^4}{4!} + \dots$$

FORMULAE LIST (continued)

De Moivre's theorem

$$[r(\cos\theta + i\sin\theta)]^n = r^n(\cos n\theta + i\sin n\theta)$$

Vector product

$$\mathbf{a}\times\mathbf{b} = |\mathbf{a}||\mathbf{b}|\sin\theta\,\hat{\mathbf{n}} = \begin{vmatrix} \mathbf{i} & \mathbf{j} & \mathbf{k} \\ a_1 & a_2 & a_3 \\ b_1 & b_2 & b_3 \end{vmatrix} = \mathbf{i}\begin{vmatrix} a_2 & a_3 \\ b_2 & b_3 \end{vmatrix} - \mathbf{j}\begin{vmatrix} a_1 & a_3 \\ b_1 & b_3 \end{vmatrix} + \mathbf{k}\begin{vmatrix} a_1 & a_2 \\ b_1 & b_2 \end{vmatrix}$$

Matrix transformation

Anti-clockwise rotation through an angle, θ, about the origin, $\begin{pmatrix} \cos\theta & -\sin\theta \\ \sin\theta & \cos\theta \end{pmatrix}$

Total marks — 100

MARKS

Attempt ALL questions

1. (a) Given $f(x) = (x + 1)(x - 2)^3$, obtain the values of x for which $f'(x) = 0$.   3

    (b) Calculate the gradient of the curve defined by $\dfrac{x^2}{y} + x = y - 5$ at the point $(3, -1)$.   4

2. The first term of an arithmetic sequence is 2 and the 20th term is 97. Obtain the sum of the first 50 terms.   4

3. Show that $z = 3 + 3i$ is a root of the equation $z^3 - 18z + 108 = 0$ and obtain the remaining roots of the equation.   4

4. Let the matrix $A = \begin{pmatrix} 1 & x \\ x & 4 \end{pmatrix}$.

    (a) Obtain the value(s) of x for which A is singular.   2

    (b) When $x = 2$, show that $A^2 = pA$ for some constant p.

    Determine the value of q such that $A^4 = qA$.   3

5. (a) Write down the binomial expansion of $(1 + x)^5$.   1

    (b) Hence show that $0 \cdot 9^5$ is $0 \cdot 59049$.   2

6. Use the substitution $x = 1 + \sin\theta$ to evaluate $\displaystyle\int_0^{\frac{\pi}{2}} \frac{\cos\theta}{(1 + \sin\theta)^3} \, d\theta$.   5

7. Obtain the first three non-zero terms in the Maclaurin expansion of $(1 + \sin^2 x)$.   4

8. Prove by induction that, for all positive integers n,

    $$\sum_{r=1}^{n} \frac{1}{r(r+1)} = 1 - \frac{1}{n+1}.$$ 5

MARKS

9. Given that $y > -1$ and $x > -1$, obtain the general solution of the differential equation

$$\frac{dy}{dx} = 3(1+y)\sqrt{1+x},$$

expressing your answer in the form $y = f(x)$.   **5**

10. Use integration by parts to obtain the exact value of $\int_0^1 x\tan^{-1}x^2\,dx$.   **5**

11. A body moves along a straight line with velocity $v = t^3 - 12t^2 + 32t$ at time t.

(a) Obtain the value of its acceleration when $t = 0$.   **1**

(b) At time $t = 0$, the body is at the origin O.

Obtain a formula for the displacement of the body at time t.

Show that the body returns to O, and obtain the time, T, when this happens.   **4**

12. Given that $|z - 2| = |z + i|$, where $z = x + iy$, show that $ax + by + c = 0$ for suitable values of a, b and c.

Indicate on an Argand diagram the locus of complex numbers z which satisfy $|z - 2| = |z + i|$.   **4**

13. Prove by contradiction that if x is an irrational number, then $2 + x$ is irrational.   **4**

14. Obtain the general solution of the differential equation

$$\frac{d^2y}{dx^2} - 3\frac{dy}{dx} + 2y = 2x^2.$$

Given that $y = \frac{1}{2}$ and $\frac{dy}{dx} = 1$ when $x = 0$, find the particular solution.   **10**

MARKS

15. Express $\dfrac{1}{x^3 + x}$ in partial fractions.

Obtain a formula for $I(k)$, where $I(k) = \displaystyle\int_1^k \dfrac{1}{x^3 + x}\,dx$, expressing it in the form $\ln\dfrac{a}{b}$, where a and b depend on k.

Write down an expression for $e^{I(k)}$ and obtain the value of $\lim_{k\to\infty} e^{I(k)}$.   **10**

16. Let $f(x) = \dfrac{x}{\ln x}$ for $x > 1$.

(a) Derive expressions for $f'(x)$ and $f''(x)$, simplifying your answers.   **4**

(b) Obtain the coordinates and nature of the stationary point of the curve $y = f(x)$.   **3**

(c) Obtain the coordinates of the point of inflexion.   **2**

17. (a) Use Gaussian elimination on the following system of equations to give an expression for z in terms of λ.

$$x + y - z = 6$$
$$2x - 3y + 2z = 2$$
$$-5x + 2y + \lambda z = 1$$

Determine the solution to this system of equations when $\lambda = -4$.   **5**

(b) Show that the line of intersection, L, of the planes $x + y - z = 6$ and $2x - 3y + 2z = 2$ has parametric equations

$$x = t$$
$$y = 4t - 14$$
$$z = 5t - 20.$$ **2**

(c) Find the acute angle between line L and the plane $-5x + 2y - 4z = 1$.   **4**

[END OF MODEL PAPER]

ADVANCED HIGHER

2016

National Qualifications 2016

X747/77/11

Mathematics

THURSDAY, 12 MAY
9:00 AM — 12:00 NOON

Total marks — 100

Attempt ALL questions.

You may use a calculator.

Full credit will be given only to solutions which contain appropriate working.

State the units for your answer where appropriate.

Answers obtained by readings from scale drawings will not receive any credit.

Write your answers clearly in the answer booklet provided. In the answer booklet, you must clearly identify the question number you are attempting.

Use **blue** or **black** ink.

Before leaving the examination room you must give your answer booklet to the Invigilator; if you do not, you may lose all the marks for this paper.

FORMULAE LIST

Standard derivatives	
$f(x)$	$f'(x)$
$\sin^{-1}x$	$\dfrac{1}{\sqrt{1-x^2}}$
$\cos^{-1}x$	$-\dfrac{1}{\sqrt{1-x^2}}$
$\tan^{-1}x$	$\dfrac{1}{1+x^2}$
$\tan x$	$\sec^2 x$
$\cot x$	$-\operatorname{cosec}^2 x$
$\sec x$	$\sec x \tan x$
$\operatorname{cosec} x$	$-\operatorname{cosec} x \cot x$
$\ln x$	$\dfrac{1}{x}$
e^x	e^x

Standard integrals	
$f(x)$	$\int f(x)\,dx$
$\sec^2(ax)$	$\dfrac{1}{a}\tan(ax)+c$
$\dfrac{1}{\sqrt{a^2-x^2}}$	$\sin^{-1}\left(\dfrac{x}{a}\right)+c$
$\dfrac{1}{a^2+x^2}$	$\dfrac{1}{a}\tan^{-1}\left(\dfrac{x}{a}\right)+c$
$\dfrac{1}{x}$	$\ln|x|+c$
e^{ax}	$\dfrac{1}{a}e^{ax}+c$

Summations

(Arithmetic series) $S_n = \dfrac{1}{2}n[2a+(n-1)d]$

(Geometric series) $S_n = \dfrac{a(1-r^n)}{1-r}, r \neq 1$

$$\sum_{r=1}^{n} r = \frac{n(n+1)}{2}, \quad \sum_{r=1}^{n} r^2 = \frac{n(n+1)(2n+1)}{6}, \quad \sum_{r=1}^{n} r^3 = \frac{n^2(n+1)^2}{4}$$

Binomial theorem

$$(a+b)^n = \sum_{r=0}^{n} \binom{n}{r} a^{n-r} b^r \text{ where } \binom{n}{r} = {}^nC_r = \frac{n!}{r!(n-r)!}$$

Maclaurin expansion

$$f(x) = f(0) + f'(0)x + \frac{f''(0)x^2}{2!} + \frac{f'''(0)x^3}{3!} + \frac{f^{iv}(0)x^4}{4!} + \dots$$

FORMULAE LIST (continued)

De Moivre's theorem

$$[r(\cos\theta + i\sin\theta)]^n = r^n(\cos n\theta + i\sin n\theta)$$

Vector product

$$\mathbf{a}\times\mathbf{b} = |\mathbf{a}||\mathbf{b}|\sin\theta\,\hat{\mathbf{n}} = \begin{vmatrix} \mathbf{i} & \mathbf{j} & \mathbf{k} \\ a_1 & a_2 & a_3 \\ b_1 & b_2 & b_3 \end{vmatrix} = \mathbf{i}\begin{vmatrix} a_2 & a_3 \\ b_2 & b_3 \end{vmatrix} - \mathbf{j}\begin{vmatrix} a_1 & a_3 \\ b_1 & b_3 \end{vmatrix} + \mathbf{k}\begin{vmatrix} a_1 & a_2 \\ b_1 & b_2 \end{vmatrix}$$

Matrix transformation

Anti-clockwise rotation through an angle, θ, about the origin, $\begin{pmatrix} \cos\theta & -\sin\theta \\ \sin\theta & \cos\theta \end{pmatrix}$

[Turn over

Total marks — 100

MARKS

Attempt ALL questions

1. (a) Differentiate $y = x\tan^{-1}2x$.　3

   (b) Given $f(x) = \dfrac{1-x^2}{1+4x^2}$, find $f'(x)$, simplifying your answer.　3

   (c) A curve is given by the parametric equations

   $$x = 6t \text{ and } y = 1 - \cos t.$$

   Find $\dfrac{dy}{dx}$ in terms of t.　2

2. A geometric sequence has second and fifth terms 108 and 4 respectively.

   (a) Calculate the value of the common ratio.　3

   (b) State why the associated geometric series has a sum to infinity.　1

   (c) Find the value of this sum to infinity.　2

3. Write down and simplify the general term in the binomial expansion of $\left(\dfrac{3}{x} - 2x\right)^{13}$.

   Hence, or otherwise, find the term in x^9.　5

4. Below is a system of equations:

   $$x + 2y + 3z = 3$$
   $$2x - y + 4z = 5$$
   $$x - 3y + 2\lambda z = 2$$

   Use Gaussian elimination to find the value of λ which leads to redundancy.　4

5. Prove **by induction** that

   $$\sum_{r=1}^{n} r(3r-1) = n^2(n+1), \qquad \forall n \in \mathbb{N}.$$　4

MARKS

6. Find Maclaurin expansions for $\sin 3x$ and e^{4x} up to and including the term in x^3.

   Hence obtain an expansion for $e^{4x}\sin 3x$ up to and including the term in x^3.   **6**

7. A is the matrix $\begin{pmatrix} 2 & 0 \\ \lambda & -1 \end{pmatrix}$.

   (a) Find the determinant of matrix A.   **1**

   (b) Show that A^2 can be expressed in the form $pA+qI$, stating the values of p and q.   **3**

   (c) Obtain a similar expression for A^4.   **2**

8. Let $z=\sqrt{3}-i$.

   (a) Plot z on an Argand diagram.   **1**

   (b) Let $w=az$ where $a>0$, $a\in\mathbb{R}$.

   Express w in polar form.   **2**

   (c) Express w^8 in the form $ka^n\left(x+i\sqrt{y}\right)$ where $k,x,y\in\mathbb{Z}$.   **3**

9. Obtain $\int x^7\left(\ln x\right)^2\,dx$.   **6**

10. For each of the following statements, decide whether it is true or false.

    If true, give a proof; if false, give a counterexample.

    A. If a positive integer p is prime, then so is $2p+1$.

    B. If a positive integer n has remainder 1 when divided by 3, then n^3 also has remainder 1 when divided by 3.   **4**

11. The height of a cube is increasing at the rate of $5\,\text{cm s}^{-1}$.

    Find the rate of increase of the volume when the height of the cube is $3\,\text{cm}$.   **4**

[Turn over

12. Below is a diagram showing the graph of a linear function, $y = f(x)$.

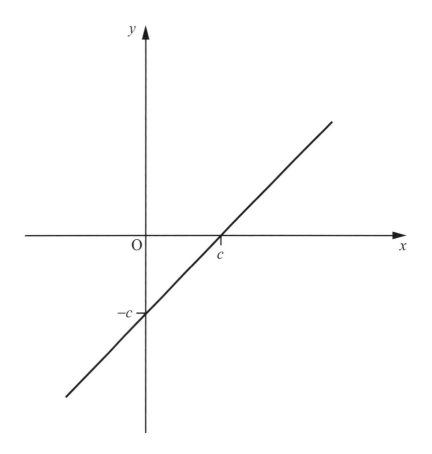

On separate diagrams show:

(a) $y = |f(x) - c|$ **2**

(b) $y = |2f(x)|$ **2**

13. Express $\dfrac{3x + 32}{(x+4)(6-x)}$ in partial fractions and hence evaluate

$$\int_{3}^{4} \frac{3x + 32}{(x+4)(6-x)}\,dx.$$

Give your answer in the form $\ln\left(\dfrac{p}{q}\right)$.   **9**

MARKS

14. Two lines L_1 and L_2 are given by the equations:

$$L_1: \quad x = 4+3\lambda, \quad y = 2+4\lambda, \quad z = -7\lambda$$

$$L_2: \quad \frac{x-3}{-2} = \frac{y-8}{1} = \frac{z+1}{3}$$

(a) Show that the lines L_1 and L_2 intersect and find the point of intersection.   5

(b) Calculate the obtuse angle between the lines L_1 and L_2.   4

15. Solve the differential equation

$$\frac{d^2y}{dx^2} + 5\frac{dy}{dx} + 6y = 12x^2 + 2x - 5$$

given $y=-6$ and $\dfrac{dy}{dx}=3$, when $x=0$.   10

16. A beaker of liquid was placed in a fridge.

The rate of cooling is given by

$$\frac{dT}{dt} = -k\left(T - T_F\right), \quad k > 0,$$

where T_F is the constant temperature in the fridge and T is the temperature of the liquid at time t.

- The constant temperature in the fridge is $4\,°C$.
- When first placed in the fridge, the temperature of the liquid was $25\,°C$.
- At 12 noon, the temperature of the liquid was $9{\cdot}8\,°C$.
- At 12:15 pm, the temperature of the liquid had dropped to $6{\cdot}5\,°C$.

At what time, to the nearest minute, was the liquid placed in the fridge?   9

[END OF QUESTION PAPER]

Page eight

[BLANK PAGE]

DO NOT WRITE ON THIS PAGE

ADVANCED HIGHER

2017

National
Qualifications
2017

X747/77/11

Mathematics

FRIDAY, 5 MAY
9:00 AM — 12:00 NOON

Total marks — 100

Attempt ALL questions.

You may use a calculator.

Full credit will be given only to solutions which contain appropriate working.

State the units for your answer where appropriate.

Answers obtained by readings from scale drawings will not receive any credit.

Write your answers clearly in the answer booklet provided. In the answer booklet, you must clearly identify the question number you are attempting.

Use **blue** or **black** ink.

Before leaving the examination room you must give your answer booklet to the Invigilator; if you do not, you may lose all the marks for this paper.

FORMULAE LIST

Standard derivatives	
$f(x)$	$f'(x)$
$\sin^{-1}x$	$\dfrac{1}{\sqrt{1-x^2}}$
$\cos^{-1}x$	$-\dfrac{1}{\sqrt{1-x^2}}$
$\tan^{-1}x$	$\dfrac{1}{1+x^2}$
$\tan x$	$\sec^2 x$
$\cot x$	$-\operatorname{cosec}^2 x$
$\sec x$	$\sec x \tan x$
$\operatorname{cosec} x$	$-\operatorname{cosec} x \cot x$
$\ln x$	$\dfrac{1}{x}$
e^x	e^x

Standard integrals	
$f(x)$	$\int f(x)\,dx$
$\sec^2(ax)$	$\dfrac{1}{a}\tan(ax)+c$
$\dfrac{1}{\sqrt{a^2-x^2}}$	$\sin^{-1}\left(\dfrac{x}{a}\right)+c$
$\dfrac{1}{a^2+x^2}$	$\dfrac{1}{a}\tan^{-1}\left(\dfrac{x}{a}\right)+c$
$\dfrac{1}{x}$	$\ln|x|+c$
e^{ax}	$\dfrac{1}{a}e^{ax}+c$

Summations

(Arithmetic series) $S_n = \dfrac{1}{2}n[2a+(n-1)d]$

(Geometric series) $S_n = \dfrac{a(1-r^n)}{1-r}, r \neq 1$

$$\sum_{r=1}^{n} r = \frac{n(n+1)}{2}, \quad \sum_{r=1}^{n} r^2 = \frac{n(n+1)(2n+1)}{6}, \quad \sum_{r=1}^{n} r^3 = \frac{n^2(n+1)^2}{4}$$

Binomial theorem

$$(a+b)^n = \sum_{r=0}^{n}\binom{n}{r}a^{n-r}b^r \text{ where } \binom{n}{r} = {}^nC_r = \frac{n!}{r!(n-r)!}$$

Maclaurin expansion

$$f(x) = f(0) + f'(0)x + \frac{f''(0)x^2}{2!} + \frac{f'''(0)x^3}{3!} + \frac{f^{iv}(0)x^4}{4!} + \ldots$$

FORMULAE LIST (continued)

De Moivre's theorem

$$\left[r(\cos\theta + i\sin\theta)\right]^{n} = r^{n}\left(\cos n\theta + i\sin n\theta\right)$$

Vector product

$$\mathbf{a}\times\mathbf{b} = |\mathbf{a}||\mathbf{b}|\sin\theta\,\hat{\mathbf{n}} = \begin{vmatrix} \mathbf{i} & \mathbf{j} & \mathbf{k} \\ a_1 & a_2 & a_3 \\ b_1 & b_2 & b_3 \end{vmatrix} = \mathbf{i}\begin{vmatrix} a_2 & a_3 \\ b_2 & b_3 \end{vmatrix} - \mathbf{j}\begin{vmatrix} a_1 & a_3 \\ b_1 & b_3 \end{vmatrix} + \mathbf{k}\begin{vmatrix} a_1 & a_2 \\ b_1 & b_2 \end{vmatrix}$$

Matrix transformation

Anti-clockwise rotation through an angle, θ, about the origin, $\begin{pmatrix} \cos\theta & -\sin\theta \\ \sin\theta & \cos\theta \end{pmatrix}$

[Turn over

Total marks — 100   MARKS

Attempt ALL questions

1. Write down the binomial expansion of $\left(\dfrac{2}{y^2}-5y\right)^3$ and simplify your answer.   4

2. Express $\dfrac{x^2-6x+20}{(x+1)(x-2)^2}$ in partial fractions.   4

3. On a suitable domain, a function is defined by $f(x)=\dfrac{e^{x^2-1}}{x^2-1}$.

   Find $f'(x)$, simplifying your answer.   3

4. The fifth term of an arithmetic sequence is −6 and the twelfth term is −34.

   (a) Determine the values of the first term and the common difference.   2

   (b) Obtain algebraically the value of n for which $S_n=-144$.   3

5. (a) (i) Use Gaussian elimination on the system of equations below to give an expression for z in terms of λ.   4

$$x+2y-z=-3$$
$$4x-2y+3z=11$$
$$3x+y+2\lambda z=8$$

   (ii) For what value of λ is this system of equations inconsistent?   1

   (b) Determine the solution of this system when $\lambda=-2\cdot5$.   1

6. Use the substitution $u=5x^2$ to find the exact value of $\displaystyle\int_0^{\frac{1}{\sqrt{10}}}\dfrac{x}{\sqrt{1-25x^4}}\,dx$.   6

MARKS

7. Matrices P and Q are defined by $P = \begin{pmatrix} x & 2 \\ -5 & -1 \end{pmatrix}$ and $Q = \begin{pmatrix} 2 & -3 \\ 4 & y \end{pmatrix}$, where $x, y \in \mathbb{R}$.

   (a) Given the determinant of P is 2, obtain:

        (i) The value of x.   1

        (ii) P^{-1}.   1

        (iii) $P^{-1}Q'$, where Q' is the transpose of Q.   2

   (b) The matrix R is defined by $R = \begin{pmatrix} 5 & -2 \\ z & -6 \end{pmatrix}$, where $z \in \mathbb{R}$.

        Determine the value of z such that R is singular.   2

8. Use the Euclidean algorithm to find integers a and b such that $1595a + 1218b = 29$.   4

9. Solve $\dfrac{dy}{dx} = e^{2x}\left(1 + y^2\right)$ given that when $x=0$, $y=1$.

   Express y in terms of x.   5

10. S_n is defined by $\displaystyle\sum_{r=1}^{n}\left(r^2 + \frac{1}{3}r\right)$.

    (a) Find an expression for S_n, fully factorising your answer.   2

    (b) Hence find an expression for $\displaystyle\sum_{r=10}^{2p}\left(r^2 + \frac{1}{3}r\right)$ where $p > 5$.   2

[Turn over

Page five

MARKS

11. Given $y = x^{2x^3+1}$, use logarithmic differentiation to find $\dfrac{dy}{dx}$.

Write your answer in terms of x.

5

12. In the diagram below part of the graph of $y = f(x)$ has been omitted.

The point $(-1, -2)$ lies on the graph and the line $y = \dfrac{1}{2}x - 3$ is an asymptote.

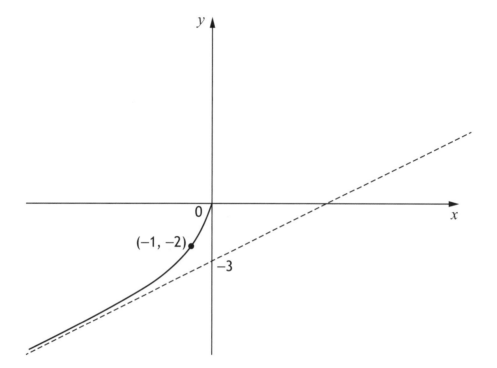

Given that $f(x)$ is an odd function:

(a) Copy and complete the diagram, including any asymptotes and any points you know to be on the graph.

2

(b) $g(x) = \left| f(x) \right|$. On a separate diagram, sketch $g(x)$.

Include known asymptotes and points.

2

(c) State the range of values of $f'(x)$ given that $f'(0) = 2$.

1

13. Let n be an integer.

Using proof by contrapositive, show that if n^2 is even, then n is even.

4

MARKS

14. Find the particular solution of the differential equation

$$\frac{d^2y}{dx^2} - 6\frac{dy}{dx} + 9y = 8\sin x + 19\cos x$$

given that $y=7$ and $\frac{dy}{dx} = \frac{1}{2}$ when $x=0$.   10

15. (a) A beam of light passes through the points B(7, 8, 1) and T(−3, −22, 6).

   Obtain parametric equations of the line representing the beam of light.   2

   (b) A sheet of metal is represented by a plane containing the points P(2, 1, 9), Q(1, 2, 7) and R(−3, 7, 1).

   Find the Cartesian equation of the plane.   4

   (c) The beam of light passes through a hole in the metal at point H.

   Find the coordinates of H.   3

16. On a suitable domain, a curve is defined by the equation $4x^2 + 9y^2 = 36$.

   A section of the curve in the first quadrant, illustrated in the diagram below, is rotated 360° about the **y-axis**.

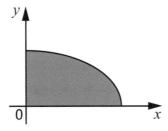

   Calculate the exact value of the volume generated.   5

[Turn over for next question

17. The complex number $z = 2 + i$ is a root of the polynomial equation
$z^4 - 6z^3 + 16z^2 - 22z + q = 0$, where $q \in \mathbb{Z}$.

MARKS

(a) State a second root of the equation.   **1**

(b) Find the value of q and the remaining roots.   **6**

(c) Show the solutions to $z^4 - 6z^3 + 16z^2 - 22z + q = 0$ on an Argand diagram.   **1**

18. The position of a particle at time t is given by the parametric equations

$x = t \cos t, \quad y = t \sin t, \quad t \geq 0$.

(a) Find an expression for the instantaneous speed of the particle.   **5**

The diagram below shows the path that the particle takes.

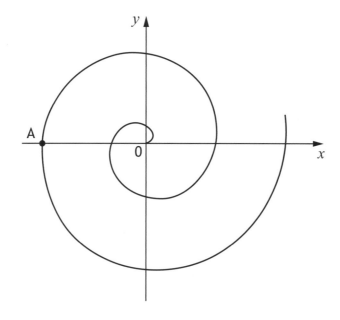

(b) Calculate the instantaneous speed of the particle at point A.   **2**

[END OF QUESTION PAPER]

ADVANCED HIGHER

2018

National
Qualifications
2018

X747/77/11

Mathematics

THURSDAY, 3 MAY
9:00 AM — 12:00 NOON

Total marks — 100

Attempt ALL questions.

You may use a calculator.

Full credit will be given only to solutions which contain appropriate working.

State the units for your answer where appropriate.

Answers obtained by readings from scale drawings will not receive any credit.

Write your answers clearly in the answer booklet provided. In the answer booklet, you must clearly identify the question number you are attempting.

Use **blue** or **black** ink.

Before leaving the examination room you must give your answer booklet to the Invigilator; if you do not, you may lose all the marks for this paper.

FORMULAE LIST

Standard derivatives	
$f(x)$	$f'(x)$
$\sin^{-1}x$	$\dfrac{1}{\sqrt{1-x^2}}$
$\cos^{-1}x$	$-\dfrac{1}{\sqrt{1-x^2}}$
$\tan^{-1}x$	$\dfrac{1}{1+x^2}$
$\tan x$	$\sec^2 x$
$\cot x$	$-\operatorname{cosec}^2 x$
$\sec x$	$\sec x \tan x$
$\operatorname{cosec} x$	$-\operatorname{cosec} x \cot x$
$\ln x$	$\dfrac{1}{x}$
e^x	e^x

Standard integrals	
$f(x)$	$\displaystyle\int f(x)\,dx$
$\sec^2(ax)$	$\dfrac{1}{a}\tan(ax)+c$
$\dfrac{1}{\sqrt{a^2-x^2}}$	$\sin^{-1}\left(\dfrac{x}{a}\right)+c$
$\dfrac{1}{a^2+x^2}$	$\dfrac{1}{a}\tan^{-1}\left(\dfrac{x}{a}\right)+c$
$\dfrac{1}{x}$	$\ln|x|+c$
e^{ax}	$\dfrac{1}{a}e^{ax}+c$

Summations

(Arithmetic series) $\qquad S_n = \dfrac{1}{2}n[2a+(n-1)d]$

(Geometric series) $\qquad S_n = \dfrac{a(1-r^n)}{1-r}, r \neq 1$

$$\sum_{r=1}^{n} r = \frac{n(n+1)}{2}, \quad \sum_{r=1}^{n} r^2 = \frac{n(n+1)(2n+1)}{6}, \quad \sum_{r=1}^{n} r^3 = \frac{n^2(n+1)^2}{4}$$

Binomial theorem

$$(a+b)^n = \sum_{r=0}^{n} \binom{n}{r} a^{n-r} b^r \text{ where } \binom{n}{r} = {}^nC_r = \frac{n!}{r!(n-r)!}$$

Maclaurin expansion

$$f(x) = f(0) + f'(0)x + \frac{f''(0)x^2}{2!} + \frac{f'''(0)x^3}{3!} + \frac{f^{iv}(0)x^4}{4!} + \dots$$

FORMULAE LIST (continued)

De Moivre's theorem

$$[r(\cos\theta + i\sin\theta)]^n = r^n(\cos n\theta + i\sin n\theta)$$

Vector product

$$\mathbf{a} \times \mathbf{b} = |\mathbf{a}||\mathbf{b}|\sin\theta\,\hat{\mathbf{n}} = \begin{vmatrix} \mathbf{i} & \mathbf{j} & \mathbf{k} \\ a_1 & a_2 & a_3 \\ b_1 & b_2 & b_3 \end{vmatrix} = \mathbf{i}\begin{vmatrix} a_2 & a_3 \\ b_2 & b_3 \end{vmatrix} - \mathbf{j}\begin{vmatrix} a_1 & a_3 \\ b_1 & b_3 \end{vmatrix} + \mathbf{k}\begin{vmatrix} a_1 & a_2 \\ b_1 & b_2 \end{vmatrix}$$

Matrix transformation

Anti-clockwise rotation through an angle, θ, about the origin, $\begin{pmatrix} \cos\theta & -\sin\theta \\ \sin\theta & \cos\theta \end{pmatrix}$

[Turn over

Page three

Total marks — 100

MARKS

Attempt ALL questions

1. (a) Given $f(x) = \sin^{-1} 3x$, find $f'(x)$. 2

   (b) Differentiate $y = \dfrac{e^{5x}}{7x+1}$. 2

   (c) For $y\cos x + y^2 = 6x$, use implicit differentiation to find $\dfrac{dy}{dx}$. 4

2. Use partial fractions to find $\displaystyle\int \frac{3x-7}{x^2 - 2x - 15}\,dx$. 4

3. (a) Write down and simplify the general term in the binomial expansion of $\left(2x + \dfrac{5}{x^2}\right)^9$. 3

   (b) Hence, or otherwise, find the term independent of x. 2

4. Given that $z_1 = 2 + 3i$ and $z_2 = p - 6i$, $p \in \mathbb{R}$, find:

   (a) $z_1 \bar{z}_2$; 2

   (b) the value of p such that $z_1 \bar{z}_2$ is a real number. 1

5. Use the Euclidean algorithm to find integers a and b such that $306a + 119b = 17$. 4

MARKS

6. On a suitable domain, a curve is defined parametrically by $x = t^2 + 1$ and $y = \ln(3t + 2)$.

   Find the equation of the tangent to the curve where $t = -\dfrac{1}{3}$. **5**

7. Matrices C and D are given by:

$$C = \begin{pmatrix} -2 & 1 & 2 \\ 1 & -1 & 0 \\ 1 & 0 & -1 \end{pmatrix} \quad \text{and} \quad D = \begin{pmatrix} 1 & 1 & 2 \\ k+3 & 0 & 2 \\ 1 & 1 & 1 \end{pmatrix}, \text{ where } k \in \mathbb{R}.$$

   (a) Obtain $2C' - D$ where C' is the transpose of C. **2**

   (b) (i) Find and simplify an expression for the determinant of D. **2**

   (ii) State the value of k such that D^{-1} does not exist. **1**

8. Using the substitution $u = \sin\theta$, or otherwise, evaluate

$$\int_{\frac{\pi}{6}}^{\frac{\pi}{2}} 2\sin^4\theta \cos\theta \, d\theta.$$ **4**

9. Prove directly that:

   (a) the sum of any three consecutive integers is divisible by 3; **2**

   (b) any odd integer can be expressed as the sum of two consecutive integers. **1**

[Turn over

MARKS

10. Given $z = x + iy$, sketch the locus in the complex plane given by $|z| = |z - 2 + 2i|$.

3

11. (a) Obtain the matrix, A, associated with an anticlockwise rotation of $\dfrac{\pi}{3}$ radians about the origin.

1

(b) Find the matrix, B, associated with a reflection in the x-axis.

1

(c) Hence obtain the matrix, P, associated with an anticlockwise rotation of $\dfrac{\pi}{3}$ radians about the origin followed by reflection in the x-axis, expressing your answer using exact values.

2

(d) Explain why matrix P is not associated with rotation about the origin.

1

12. Prove by induction that, for all positive integers n,

$$\sum_{r=1}^{n} 3^{r-1} = \frac{1}{2}\left(3^n - 1\right).$$

5

MARKS

13. An engineer has designed a lifting device. The handle turns a screw which shortens the horizontal length and increases the vertical height.

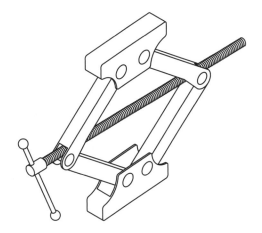

The device is modelled by a rhombus, with each side 25 cm.

The horizontal length is x cm, and the vertical height is h cm as shown.

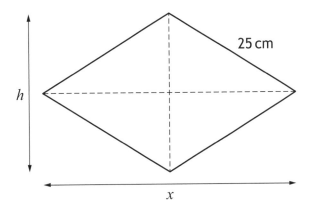

(a) Show that $h = \sqrt{2500 - x^2}$.   1

(b) The horizontal length decreases at a rate of 0·3 cm per second as the handle is turned.

Find the rate of change of the vertical height when $x = 30$.   5

[Turn over

MARKS

14. A geometric sequence has first term 80 and common ratio $\frac{1}{3}$.

(a) For this sequence, calculate:

(i) the 7th term; 2

(ii) the sum to infinity of the associated geometric series. 2

The first term of this geometric sequence is equal to the first term of an arithmetic sequence.

The sum of the first five terms of this arithmetic sequence is 240.

(b) (i) Find the common difference of this sequence. 2

(ii) Write down and simplify an expression for the nth term. 1

Let S_n represent the sum of the first n terms of this arithmetic sequence.

(c) Find the values of n for which $S_n = 144$. 3

15. (a) Use integration by parts to find $\int x \sin 3x \, dx$. 3

(b) Hence find the particular solution of

$$\frac{dy}{dx} - \frac{2}{x} y = x^3 \sin 3x, \quad x \neq 0$$

given that $x = \pi$ when $y = 0$.

Express your answer in the form $y = f(x)$. 7

MARKS

16. Planes π_1, π_2 and π_3 have equations:

$$\pi_1: \qquad x - 2y + z = -4$$
$$\pi_2: \qquad 3x - 5y - 2z = 1$$
$$\pi_3: \qquad -7x + 11y + az = -11$$

where $a \in \mathbb{R}$.

(a) Use Gaussian elimination to find the value of a such that the intersection of the planes π_1, π_2 and π_3 is a line.   **4**

(b) Find the equation of the line of intersection of the planes when a takes this value.   **2**

The plane π_4 has equation $-9x + 15y + 6z = 20$.

(c) Find the acute angle between π_1 and π_4.   **3**

(d) Describe the geometrical relationship between π_2 and π_4.

Justify your answer.   **1**

17. (a) Given $f(x) = e^{2x}$, obtain the Maclaurin expansion for $f(x)$ up to, and including, the term in x^3.   **2**

(b) On a suitable domain, let $g(x) = \tan x$.

   (i) Show that the third derivative of $g(x)$ is given by
   $$g'''(x) = 2\sec^4 x + 4\tan^2 x \sec^2 x.$$ **3**

   (ii) Hence obtain the Maclaurin expansion for $g(x)$ up to and including the term in x^3.   **2**

(c) Hence, or otherwise, obtain the Maclaurin expansion for $e^{2x}\tan x$ up to, and including, the term in x^3.   **2**

(d) Write down the first three non-zero terms in the Maclaurin expansion for $2e^{2x}\tan x + e^{2x}\sec^2 x$.   **1**

[END OF QUESTION PAPER]

Page ten

[BLANK PAGE]

DO NOT WRITE ON THIS PAGE

ADVANCED HIGHER

Answers

ADVANCED HIGHER MATHEMATICS
MODEL PAPER

Question		Expected response (Give one mark for each •)	Additional guidance (Illustration of evidence for awarding a mark at each •)	Max mark
1.	(a)	Ans: $x = 2$ and $x = -\dfrac{1}{4}$ •¹ correct use of product rule •² factorise $f'(x)$ •³ solve $f'(x) = 0$	•¹ $f'(x) = (x-2)^3 + 3(x+1)(x-2)^2$ •² $f'(x) = (x-2)^2(4x+1)$ •³ $x = 2$ and $x = -\dfrac{1}{4}$	3
	(b)	Ans: $-\dfrac{1}{2}$ **Method 1** •⁴ differentiate LHS of equation •⁵ differentiate RHS of equation •⁶ substitute for x and y or find $\dfrac{dy}{dx}$ •⁷ find gradient of curve **Method 2** •⁴ start to differentiate using quotient rule •⁵ complete differentiation •⁶ substitute for x and y or find $\dfrac{dy}{dx}$ •⁷ find gradient of curve	•⁴ $2x + x\dfrac{dy}{dx} + y = \ldots$ •⁵ $2x + x\dfrac{dy}{dx} + y = 2y\dfrac{dy}{dx} - 5\dfrac{dy}{dx}$ •⁶ $6 + 3\dfrac{dy}{dx} - 1 = -2\dfrac{dy}{dx} - 5\dfrac{dy}{dx}$ or $\dfrac{dy}{dx} = \dfrac{2x+y}{2y-x-5}$ •⁷ $5 = -10\dfrac{dy}{dx} \Rightarrow \dfrac{dy}{dx} = -\dfrac{1}{2}$ or $\dfrac{dy}{dx} = \dfrac{6-1}{-2-3-5} = \dfrac{5}{-10} = -\dfrac{1}{2}$ •⁴ $\dfrac{2xy - \ldots}{y^2}$ •⁵ $\dfrac{2xy - x^2\dfrac{dy}{dx}}{y^2} + 1 = \dfrac{dy}{dx}$ •⁶ $\dfrac{-6 - 9\dfrac{dy}{dx}}{1} + 1 = \dfrac{dy}{dx}$ or $\dfrac{dy}{dx} = \dfrac{2xy + y^2}{x^2 + y^2}$ •⁷ $-5 = 10\dfrac{dy}{dx} \Rightarrow \dfrac{dy}{dx} = -\dfrac{1}{2}$ or $\dfrac{dy}{dx} = \dfrac{-6+1}{9+1} = \dfrac{-5}{10} = -\dfrac{1}{2}$	4

Question			Expected response (Give one mark for each •)	Additional guidance (Illustration of evidence for awarding a mark at each •)	Max mark
2.			Ans: 6225		4
			•¹ use $u_n = a + (n-1)d$	•¹ $u_{20} = 97 \Rightarrow a + 19d = 97$	
			•² find d	•² $a = 2 \Rightarrow 2 + 19d = 97 \Rightarrow d = 5$	
			•³ know to use formula for S_n	•³ $S_n = \dfrac{n}{2}[2a + (n-1)d]$	
			•⁴ find S_{50}	•⁴ $\dfrac{50}{2}[4 + 49 \times 5] = 6225$	
3.			Ans: $3 - 3i$ and -6		4
			•¹ show that $3 + 3i$ is a root of the equation	•¹ $(3+3i)^3 = 27 + 81i + 81i^2 + 27i^3 = -54 + 54i$ $\Rightarrow (3+3i)^3 - 18(3+3i) + 108$ $= -54 + 54i - 54 - 54i + 108$ $= 0$	
			•² find conjugate root	•² $3 - 3i$	
			•³ find quadratic factor	•³ $(z - (3+3i))(z - (3-3i)) = z^2 - 6z + 18$	
			•⁴ find remaining root	•⁴ $z^3 - 18z + 108 = (z^2 - 6z + 18)(z + 6)$ so remaining roots are $3 - 3i$ and -6	
4.	(a)		Ans: $x = \pm 2$		2
			•¹ find determinant of matrix A	•¹ $\det A = 4 - x^2$	
			•² solve $\det A = 0$	•² $4 - x^2 = 0 \Rightarrow x = \pm 2$	
	(b)		Ans: $q = 125$		3
			•³ show that $A^2 = 5A$	•³ $A^2 = \begin{pmatrix} 1 & 2 \\ 2 & 4 \end{pmatrix}\begin{pmatrix} 1 & 2 \\ 2 & 4 \end{pmatrix} = \begin{pmatrix} 5 & 10 \\ 10 & 20 \end{pmatrix} = 5A$	
			•⁴ begin to express A^4 in terms of A	•⁴ $A^4 = (A^2)^2 = (5A)^2 = \ldots$	
			•⁵ show that $A^4 = 125A$	•⁵ $\ldots(5A)^2 = 25A^2 = 125A \Rightarrow q = 125$	
5.	(a)		Ans: $1 + 5x + 10x^2 + 10x^3 + 5x^4 + x^5$		1
			•¹ expand $(1 + x)^5$	•¹ $1 + 5x + 10x^2 + 10x^3 + 5x^4 + x^5$	
	(b)		Ans: proof		2
			•² substitute $x = -0.1$ into $(1 + x)^5$	•² $0.9^5 = (1 + (-0.1))^5$	
			•³ expand $(1 + (-0.1))^5$ and show steps leading to 0.59049	•³ $1 - 0.5 + 0.1 - 0.01 + 0.0005 - 0.00001$ $= 0.59049$	

Question	Expected response (Give one mark for each •)	Additional guidance (Illustration of evidence for awarding a mark at each •)	Max mark
6.	Ans: $\dfrac{3}{8}$ •^{1} differentiate $x = 1 + \sin\theta$ •^{2} find limits in terms of x •^{3} state integral in terms of x •^{4} integrate correctly •^{5} evaluate integral	•^{1} $x = 1 + \sin\theta \ \Rightarrow\ dx = \cos\theta\,d\theta$ •^{2} $\theta = 0 \ \Rightarrow\ x = 1$ $\theta = \dfrac{\pi}{2} \ \Rightarrow\ x = 2$ •^{3} $\displaystyle\int_{1}^{2} \dfrac{1}{x^3}\,dx$ •^{4} $\left[\dfrac{x^{-2}}{-2}\right]_{1}^{2}$ •^{5} $\dfrac{3}{8}$	5
7.	Ans: $f(x) = 1 + x^2 - \dfrac{x^4}{3}$ •^{1} evaluate $f(0)$ •^{2} evaluate $f'(0)$ and $f''(0)$ •^{3} evaluate $f'''(0)$ and $f''''(0)$ •^{4} state first three terms of $f(x)$	•^{1} $f(0) = 1$ •^{2} $f'(x) = 2\sin x \cos x = \sin 2x \ \Rightarrow\ f'(0) = 0$ $f''(x) = 2\cos 2x \ \Rightarrow\ f''(0) = 2$ •^{3} $f'''(x) = -4\sin 2x \ \Rightarrow\ f'''(0) = 0$ $f''''(x) = -8\cos 2x \ \Rightarrow\ f''''(0) = -8$ •^{4} $f(x) = 1 + x^2 - \dfrac{x^4}{3}$	4
8.	Ans: proof •^{1} show true when $n = 1$ •^{2} assume true for $n = k$ •^{3} consider $n = k + 1$ •^{4} simplify •^{5} express in required form and state conclusion	•^{1} When $n = 1$, LHS $= \dfrac{1}{1 \times 2} = \dfrac{1}{2}$, RHS $= 1 - \dfrac{1}{2} = \dfrac{1}{2}$. So true when $n = 1$. •^{2} Assume true for $n = k$, $\displaystyle\sum_{r=1}^{k} \dfrac{1}{r(r+1)} = 1 - \dfrac{1}{k+1}$ •^{3} Consider $n = k + 1$, $\displaystyle\sum_{r=1}^{k+1} \dfrac{1}{r(r+1)} = \sum_{r=1}^{k} \dfrac{1}{r(r+1)} + \dfrac{1}{(k+1)(k+2)}$ •^{4} $= 1 - \dfrac{1}{k+1} + \dfrac{1}{(k+1)(k+2)}$ $= 1 - \dfrac{k+2-1}{(k+1)(k+2)}$ $= 1 - \dfrac{k+1}{(k+1)((k+1)+1)}$ •^{5} $= 1 - \dfrac{1}{((k+1)+1)}$ Thus, if true for $n = k$, statement is true for $n = k + 1$, and, since true for $n = 1$, true for all $n \geq 1$.	5

Question	Expected response (Give one mark for each •)	Additional guidance (Illustration of evidence for awarding a mark at each •)	Max mark
9.	Ans: $y = A\exp\left(2(1+x)^{\frac{3}{2}}\right) - 1$		5
	Method 1		
	•^{1} separate the variables	•^{1} $\displaystyle\int \frac{dy}{1+y} = 3\int (1+x)^{\frac{1}{2}}\,dx$	
	•^{2} integrate term in y	•^{2} $\ln(1+y) = \ldots$	
	•^{3} integrate term in x	•^{3} $\ln(1+y) = 2(1+x)^{\frac{3}{2}} + \ldots$	
	•^{4} insert constant and eliminate ln	•^{4} $1+y = \exp\left(2(1+x)^{\frac{3}{2}} + c\right)$	
	•^{5} solve for y	•^{5} $y = \exp\left(2(1+x)^{\frac{3}{2}} + c\right) - 1$ $= A\exp\left(2(1+x)^{\frac{3}{2}}\right) - 1$	
	Method 2		
	•^{1} express in form $\dfrac{dy}{dx} + P(x)y = Q(x)$	•^{1} $\dfrac{dy}{dx} - 3\left(\sqrt{1+x}\right)y = 3\sqrt{1+x}$	
	•^{2} find integrating factor	•^{2} $\exp\left(-3\int\sqrt{1+x}\,dx\right) = \exp\left(-2(1+x)^{\frac{3}{2}}\right)$	
	•^{3} express as derivative of product	•^{3} $\dfrac{d}{dx}y\exp\left(-2(1+x)^{\frac{3}{2}}\right)$ $= 3\sqrt{1+x}\exp\left(-2(1+x)^{\frac{3}{2}}\right)$	
	•^{4} integrate	•^{4} $y\exp\left(-2(1+x)^{\frac{3}{2}}\right)$ $= -\int\left(-3\sqrt{1+x}\right)\exp\left(-2(1+x)^{\frac{3}{2}}\right)dx$ $= -\exp\left(-2(1+x)^{\frac{3}{2}}\right) + c$	
	•^{5} solve for y	•^{5} $y = -1 + c\exp\left(2(1+x)^{\frac{3}{2}}\right)$	

Question			Expected response (Give one mark for each •)	Additional guidance (Illustration of evidence for awarding a mark at each •)	Max mark
10.			Ans: $\dfrac{\pi}{8}-\dfrac{1}{4}\ln 2$ •[1] start to integrate by parts •[2] continue to integrate by parts •[3] integrate correctly •[4] substitute limits •[5] evaluate integral	•[1] $\left[\tan^{-1}x^2\int x\ dx\right]_0^1 \ldots$ •[2] $\ldots -\displaystyle\int_0^1 \dfrac{x^3}{1+x^4}\,dx$ •[3] $\left[\dfrac{1}{2}x^2\tan^{-1}x^2\right]_0^1 - \left[\dfrac{1}{4}\ln(1+x^4)\right]_0^1$ •[4] $\dfrac{1}{2}\tan^{-1}1-0-\left(\dfrac{1}{4}\ln 2-\dfrac{1}{4}\ln 1\right)$ •[5] $\dfrac{\pi}{8}-\dfrac{1}{4}\ln 2$	5
11.	(a)		Ans: 32 •[1] find acceleration when $t=0$	•[1] $a=\dfrac{dv}{dt}=3t^2-24t+32$ $\Rightarrow$ when $t=0$, $a=32$	1
	(b)		Ans: $s=\dfrac{1}{4}t^4-4t^3+16t^2$; $t=8$ •[2] integrate to find general formula for displacement •[3] find formula for displacement when $t=0$ •[4] set displacement equal to 0 and factorise •[5] state time that body returns to O	•[2] $s=\displaystyle\int t^3-12t^2+32t\,dt=\dfrac{1}{4}t^4-4t^3+16t^2+c$ •[3] $s=0$ when $t=0 \Rightarrow c=0$ $\Rightarrow s=\dfrac{1}{4}t^4-4t^3+16t^2$ •[4] at O, $s=0 \Rightarrow \dfrac{1}{4}t^4-4t^3+16t^2=0$ $\Leftrightarrow \dfrac{1}{4}t^2(t^2-16t+64)=0$ $\Leftrightarrow \dfrac{1}{4}t^2(t-8)^2=0$ •[5] the body returns to O when $t=8$	4

Question	Expected response (Give one mark for each •)	Additional guidance (Illustration of evidence for awarding a mark at each •)	Max mark
12.	Ans: $a = 4$, $b = 2$, $c = -3$; diagram		4
	•[1] substitute $z = x + iy$ into given equation	•[1] $\|z - 2\| = \|z + i\|$ $\Leftrightarrow \|(x - 2) + iy\| = \|x + (y + 1)i\|$	
	•[2] find expressions for the square of each modulus	•[2] $(x - 2)^2 + y^2 = x^2 + (y + 1)^2$	
	•[3] rearrange into the form $ax + by + c = 0$	•[3] $x^2 - 4x + 4 + y^2 = x^2 + y^2 + 2y + 1$ $\Leftrightarrow 4x + 2y - 3 = 0$	
	•[4] show locus on Argand diagram	•[4]	
13.	Ans: proof		4
	•[1] state assumption that $2 + x$ is rational	•[1] Assume $2 + x$ is rational	
	•[2] express $2 + x$ as a rational number	•[2] and let $2 + x = \dfrac{p}{q}$ where p, q are integers.	
	•[3] rearrange to express x as a rational number	•[3] So $x = \dfrac{p}{q} - 2 = \dfrac{p - 2q}{q}$.	
	•[4] state conclusion	•[4] Since $p - 2q$ and q are integers, it follows that x is rational. This is a contradiction.	

Question			Expected response (Give one mark for each •)	Additional guidance (Illustration of evidence for awarding a mark at each •)	Max mark
14.			Ans: $y = -4e^x + e^{2x} + x^2 + 3x + \dfrac{7}{2}$		10
			•[1] state the auxiliary equation	•[1] $m^2 - 3m + 2 = 0$	
			•[2] solve the auxiliary equation	•[2] $(m-1)(m-2) = 0 \Rightarrow m = 1$ or $m = 2$	
			•[3] state the complementary function	•[3] $y = Ae^x + Be^{2x}$	
			•[4] use correct form of particular integral	•[4] $y = ax^2 + bx + c$	
			•[5] substitute for $\dfrac{d^2y}{dx^2}, \dfrac{dy}{dx}$ and y in the differential equation	•[5] $\dfrac{dy}{dx} = 2ax + b, \dfrac{d^2y}{dx^2} = 2a$ $\Rightarrow 2a - 3(2ax+b) + 2(ax^2+bx+c) = 2x^2$	
			•[6] find values of a, b and c	•[6] $\Leftrightarrow 2ax^2 + (-6a+2b)x + (2a-3b+2c) = 2x^2$ $\Rightarrow a = 1, \ b = 3, \ c = \dfrac{7}{2}$	
			•[7] state general solution	•[7] $y = Ae^x + Be^{2x} + x^2 + 3x + \dfrac{7}{2}$	
			•[8] obtain equation in A and B by substituting $x = 0, \ y = \dfrac{1}{2}$ and $\dfrac{dy}{dx} = 1$ into the general solution	•[8] $\dfrac{1}{2} = A + B + \dfrac{7}{2} \Rightarrow A + B = -3$	
			•[9] obtain equation in A and B by substituting $x = 0, \ y = \dfrac{1}{2}$ and $\dfrac{dy}{dx} = 1$ into the derivative of the general solution	•[9] $\dfrac{dy}{dx} = Ae^x + 2Be^{2x} + 2x + 3$ $\Rightarrow 1 = A + 2B + 3$ $\Rightarrow A + 2B = -2$	
			•[10] state particular solution	•[10] $A = -4, \ B = 1$ $\Rightarrow y = -4e^x + e^{2x} + x^2 + 3x + \dfrac{7}{2}$	

Question	Expected response (Give one mark for each •)	Additional guidance (Illustration of evidence for awarding a mark at each •)	Max mark
15.	Ans: $\sqrt{2}$ •^{1} correct form of partial fractions •^{2} find value of A •^{3} set up equations in B and C •^{4} express integral in partial fractions •^{5} integrate first fraction •^{6} integrate second fraction •^{7} substitute limits •^{8} express integral in required form •^{9} state expression for $e^{I(k)}$ •^{10} evaluate $\lim_{k\to\infty} e^{I(k)}$	•^{1} $\dfrac{A}{x}+\dfrac{Bx+C}{x^2+1}$ •^{2} $1=A(x^2+1)+(Bx+C)x$ $\quad x=0 \;\Rightarrow\; A=1$ •^{3} $x=1 \;\Rightarrow\; 1=2+B+C$ $\quad x=-1 \;\Rightarrow\; 1=2+B-C$ •^{4} $B=-1,\; C=0$ $\Rightarrow I(k)=\displaystyle\int_1^k\left(\dfrac{1}{x}-\dfrac{x}{x^2+1}\right)dx$ •^{5} $\displaystyle\int_1^k \dfrac{1}{x}\,dx=[\ln x]_1^k$ •^{6} $\dfrac{1}{2}\displaystyle\int_1^k \dfrac{2x}{x^2+1}=\dfrac{1}{2}[\ln(x^2+1)]_1^k$ •^{7} $\ln k-\ln 1-\dfrac{1}{2}\ln(k^2+1)+\dfrac{1}{2}\ln 2$ •^{8} $\ln\dfrac{k\sqrt{2}}{\sqrt{k^2+1}}$ •^{9} $\dfrac{k\sqrt{2}}{\sqrt{k^2+1}}$ •^{10} $\dfrac{\sqrt{2}}{\sqrt{1+k^{-2}}} \to \sqrt{2}$ as $k\to\infty$	10
16. (a)	Ans: $f'(x)=\dfrac{\ln x-1}{(\ln x)^2}$ $\quad f''(x)=\dfrac{2-\ln x}{x(\ln x)^3}$ •^{1} start to use quotient rule to find $f'(x)$ •^{2} find $f'(x)$ in simplest form •^{3} use quotient rule to find $f''(x)$ •^{4} find $f''(x)$ in simplest form	•^{1} $\dfrac{1\times\ln x-\ldots}{(\ln x)^2}$ •^{2} $\dfrac{1\times\ln x-x\times\dfrac{1}{x}}{(\ln x)^2}=\dfrac{\ln x-1}{(\ln x)^2}$ •^{3} $\dfrac{\dfrac{1}{x}\times(\ln x)^2-(\ln x-1)\times\dfrac{2\ln x}{x}}{(\ln x)^4}$ •^{4} $\dfrac{\ln x-2\ln x+2}{x(\ln x)^3}=\dfrac{2-\ln x}{x(\ln x)^3}$	4

Question			Expected response (Give one mark for each •)	Additional guidance (Illustration of evidence for awarding a mark at each •)	Max mark
16.	(b)		Ans: (e, e); minimum turning point		3
			•^{5} find coordinates of stationary point	•^{5} $f'(x) = 0$ when $\ln x = 1$ $\Rightarrow$ $x = e$ and $y = e$	
			•^{6} find sign of f'' at stationary point	•^{6} At (e, e), $f''(e) = \dfrac{2-1}{e \times 1^3} > 0$	
			•^{7} state nature of stationary point	•^{7} hence (e, e) is a minimum turning point.	
	(c)		Ans: $\left(e^2, \dfrac{1}{2}e^2\right)$		2
			•^{8} find x coordinate of the point of inflexion	•^{8} $f''(x) = 0$ when $\ln x = 2$ $\Rightarrow$ $x = e^2$	
			•^{9} state the coordinates of the point of inflexion	•^{9} $x = e^2$ $\Rightarrow$ $y = \dfrac{1}{2}e^2$, so the point of inflexion is $\left(e^2, \dfrac{1}{2}e^2\right)$	
17.	(a)		Ans: $x = 3$, $y = -2$, $z = -5$		5
			•^{1} set up augmented matrix	•^{1} $\begin{array}{ccc|c} 1 & 1 & -1 & 6 \\ 2 & -3 & 2 & 2 \\ -5 & 2 & \lambda & 1 \end{array}$	
			•^{2} eliminate the x terms from rows 2 and 3	•^{2} $\Rightarrow \begin{array}{ccc|c} 1 & 1 & -1 & 6 \\ 0 & -5 & 4 & -10 \\ 0 & 7 & \lambda-5 & 31 \end{array}$	
			•^{3} eliminate the y term from row 3	•^{3} $\Rightarrow \begin{array}{ccc|c} 1 & 1 & -1 & 6 \\ 0 & -5 & 4 & -10 \\ 0 & 0 & 5\lambda+3 & 85 \end{array}$	
			•^{4} solve for z	•^{4} $z = \dfrac{85}{5\lambda+3}$	
			•^{5} solve for x and y	•^{5} $z = -5$ $-5y - 20 = -10 \Rightarrow y = -2$ $x - 2 + 5 = 6 \Rightarrow x = 3$	

Question			Expected response (Give one mark for each •)	Additional guidance (Illustration of evidence for awarding a mark at each •)	Max mark
17.	(b)		Ans: proof		2
			$\bullet^6$ eliminate y and z in system of equations	$\bullet^6$ $\begin{aligned} x + y - z &= 6 \quad (1) \\ 2x - 3y + 2z &= 2 \quad (2) \\ 5x \quad\;\; - z &= 20 \;\; (2) + 3\,(1) \\ 4x - y \quad\;\; &= 14 \;\; (2) + 2\,(1) \end{aligned}$	
			$\bullet^7$ use equations to show that $y = 4t - 14$ and $z = 5t - 20$ given that $x = t$	$\bullet^7$ $\begin{aligned} y &= 4x - 14 \\ z &= 5x - 20 \\ x &= t,\; y = 4t - 14,\; z = 5t - 20 \end{aligned}$	
	(c)		Ans: $23 \cdot 0°$		4
			$\bullet^8$ know how to find angle between the line and the plane	$\bullet^8$ evidence of $\cos\theta = \dfrac{l \cdot n}{|l||n|}$ where $\theta =$ the angle between the line and the plane, $l =$ the direction of the line and $n =$ the direction of the normal to the plane.	
			$\bullet^9$ find $l \cdot n$, $|l|$ and $|n|$	$\bullet^9$ $l = i + 4j + 5k$ and $n = -5i + 2j - 4k$ $\Rightarrow \cos\theta = \dfrac{l \cdot n}{|l||n|} = \dfrac{-17}{\sqrt{42}\sqrt{45}}$	
			$\bullet^{10}$ find angle between the line and the normal to the plane	$\bullet^{10}$ $113 \cdot 0°$	
			$\bullet^{11}$ find acute angle between the line and the plane	$\bullet^{11}$ $113 \cdot 0° - 90° = 23 \cdot 0°$	

ADVANCED HIGHER MATHEMATICS
2016

Question		Generic scheme	Illustrative scheme	Max mark
1.	(a)	$\bullet^1$ evidence of use of product rule[1,2]	$\bullet^1$ $(\ldots)\tan^{-1}2x + x(\ldots)$	3
		$\bullet^2$ one resultant term of the product correct	$\bullet^2$ $1.\tan^{-1}2x$ or $x.\dfrac{1}{1+(2x)^2}.2$	
		$\bullet^3$ complete differentiation[3]	$\bullet^3$ $\tan^{-1}2x + \dfrac{2x}{1+4x^2}$	

Notes:
1. Evidence for the award of $\bullet^1$ should take the form $f(x)\times(\ldots)+g(x)\times(\ldots)$.
2. For a candidate who interprets $\tan^{-1}2x$ as $(\tan 2x)^{-1}$ $\bullet^3$ is not available.
3. Accept $(2x)^2$ when awarding $\bullet^3$.

	(b)	$\bullet^4$ evidence of use of quotient or product rule and one term of numerator correct	$\bullet^4$ $(-2x)(1+4x^2) -$	3
		$\bullet^5$ complete differentiation correctly	$\bullet^5$ $\dfrac{\ldots(1-x^2).8x}{(1+4x^2)^2}$	
		$\bullet^6$ simplify answer[4,5]	$\bullet^6$ $-\dfrac{10x}{(1+4x^2)^2}$ or $\dfrac{-10x}{(1+4x^2)^2}$	

Notes:
4. Where a candidate uses the product rule, simplification to $-\dfrac{10x}{(1+4x^2)^2}$ or $-10x(1+4x^2)^{-2}$ will be required in order to obtain $\bullet^6$.

5. Incorrect working subsequent to a correct answer should be penalised in this instance e.g. an incorrect expansion of the denominator.

| | (c) | $\bullet^7$ correct derivatives | $\bullet^7$ 6 and $\sin t$ | 2 |
| | | $\bullet^8$ find $\dfrac{dy}{dx}$ | $\bullet^8$ $\dfrac{1}{6}\sin t$ | |

Question		Generic scheme	Illustrative scheme	Max mark
2.	(a)	•[1] interpret geometric series	•[1] $ar = 108$ and $ar^4 = 4$	3
		•[2] evidence of strategy[1,2]	•[2] $\dfrac{ar^4}{ar}$ $r^3 = \dfrac{1}{27}$	
		•[3] value[2]	•[3] $r = \dfrac{1}{3}$	

Notes:
1. For $\square$[2] accept $r^3 = \dfrac{1}{27}$.
2. For a statement of the answer only, award •[1] and •[3]. To earn •[2] there must be evidence of a strategy e.g. $108 \rightarrow 36 \rightarrow 12 \rightarrow 4$ gives $r = \dfrac{1}{3}$.

| | (b) | •[4] know condition[3,4] | •[4] $-1 < \dfrac{1}{3} < 1$ | 1 |

Notes:
3. For •[4] $\dfrac{1}{3}$ may be replaced with a letter consistent with their answer to (a). However, in the case where a candidate obtains a value in (a) outside the open interval $(-1, 1)$ •[4] will only be available where they also acknowledge that there is no sum to infinity.
4. Only award •[4] for a strict inequality, whether it is expressed algebraically or in words.

| | (c) | •[5] calculate the first term | •[5] $a = 324$ | 2 |
| | | •[6] value[5,6] | •[6] $\dfrac{324}{1 - \dfrac{1}{3}}$ or equivalent leading to 486 | |

Notes:
5. For an incorrect value in (a) •[6] will only be available provided the value satisfies the condition for convergence.
6. Where a candidate has used $S_\infty = \dfrac{a(1 - r^\infty)}{1 - r}$ full credit is available.

Question	Generic scheme	Illustrative scheme	Max mark
3.	$\bullet^1$ state general term[2]	$\bullet^1$ $^{13}C_r\left(\dfrac{3}{x}\right)^{13-r}(-2x)^r$	5
	$\bullet^2$ simplify powers of x OR coefficients **and** signs[2,5]	$\bullet^2$ $(3)^{13-r}(-2)^r$ or x^{2r-13}	
	$\bullet^3$ state simplified general term (completes simplification)[2,5]	$\bullet^3$ $^{13}C_r(3)^{13-r}(-2)^r x^{2r-13}$	
	$\bullet^4$ determine value of r[3,4]	$\bullet^4$ $2r-13=9 \Rightarrow r=11$	
	$\bullet^5$ evaluate term[1,3]	$\bullet^5$ $-1437696x^9$	

Notes:
1. Accept -1437696.
2. For $\bullet^1$ accept the initial appearance of $\displaystyle\sum_{r=0}^{13} {}^{13}C_r\left(\dfrac{3}{x}\right)^{13-r}(-2x)^r$ as bad form. $\bullet^2$ and $\bullet^3$ are available only to candidates who simplify a general term correctly.
3. $\bullet^4$ and $\bullet^5$ are the only marks available to candidates who have not proceeded from a general term e.g. an expansion using Pascal's Triangle. The required term must be explicitly identified in order for $\bullet^5$ to be awarded.
4. Starting with $^{13}C_r\left(\dfrac{3}{x}\right)^r(-2x)^{13-r}$ leading to $r=2$ can also gain full credit.
5. Accept $\dfrac{1}{x^{13-2r}}$ when awarding $\bullet^2$ or $\bullet^3$.

Question	Generic scheme	Illustrative scheme	Max mark
4.	$\bullet^1$ construct augmented matrix	$\bullet^1$ $\begin{pmatrix} 1 & 2 & 3 & \vdots & 3 \\ 2 & -1 & 4 & \vdots & 5 \\ 1 & -3 & 2\lambda & \vdots & 2 \end{pmatrix}$	4
	$\bullet^2$ use row operations to establish first two zero elements[1]	$\bullet^2$ $\begin{pmatrix} 1 & 2 & 3 & \vdots & 3 \\ 0 & 5 & 2 & \vdots & 1 \\ 0 & -5 & 2\lambda-3 & \vdots & -1 \end{pmatrix}$	
	$\bullet^3$ establish third zero element **OR** recognise linear relationship between two rows[1,2]	$\bullet^3$ $\begin{pmatrix} 1 & 2 & 3 & \vdots & 3 \\ 0 & 5 & 2 & \vdots & 1 \\ 0 & 0 & 2\lambda-1 & \vdots & 0 \end{pmatrix}$ or $2\lambda-3=-2$	
	$\bullet^4$ state value of λ[2]	$\bullet^4$ $\lambda=\dfrac{1}{2}$	

Notes:
1. Elementary row operations must be carried out correctly for $\bullet^2$ and $\bullet^3$ to be awarded.
2. $\bullet^4$ is only available where a candidate's final matrix exhibits redundancy.
3. Disregard any working/statement subsequent to $\lambda=\dfrac{1}{2}$.

Question			Generic scheme	Illustrative scheme	Max mark
5.			**PROOF**	**PROOF**	4
			$\bullet^1$ show true for $n = 1^1$	$\bullet^1$ LHS: $1(3-1) = 2$ RHS: $1^2(1+1) = 2$ So true for $n = 1$	
			$\bullet^2$ assume true for $n = k^2$ **and** consider $n = k+1$	$\bullet^2$ $\displaystyle\sum_{r=1}^{k} r(3r-1) = k^2(k+1)$ **and** $\displaystyle\sum_{r=1}^{k+1} r(3r-1) =$ $\displaystyle \ldots = \sum_{r=1}^{k} r(3r-1) + (k+1)(3(k+1)-1)$	
			$\bullet^3$ correct statement of sum to $(k+1)$ terms using inductive hypothesis	$\bullet^3$ $= k^2(k+1) + (k+1)(3k+2)$ $= (k+1)[k^2 + 3k + 2]$ $= (k+1)(k+1)(k+2)$	
			$\bullet^4$ express explicitly in terms of $(k+1)$ **or** achieve stated aim/goal[3,4] **and** communicate	$\bullet^4$ $= (k+1)^2((k+1)+1)$, thus if true for $n = k$, then true for $n = k+1$, but since true for $n = 1$, then by induction true for all $n \in \mathbb{N}$.	

Notes:

1. "RHS = 2, LHS = 2" and/or "True for $n = 1$" are insufficient for the award of $\bullet^1$. A candidate must demonstrate evidence of substitution into both expressions.

2. For $\bullet^2$ acceptable phrases include: "If true for..."; "Suppose true for..."; "Assume true for...". However, **not** acceptable: "Consider $n = k$", "assume $n = k$" and "True for $n = k$". **Allow if appears at conclusion.**

3. Full marks are available to candidates who state an aim/goal earlier in the proof and who subsequently achieve the stated aim/goal.

4. Minimum acceptable form for $\bullet^4$: "Then true for $n = k+1$, but since true for $n = 1$, then true for all n" or equivalent.

Question	Generic scheme	Illustrative scheme	Max mark
6.	**Method 1**		6
	$\bullet^1$ for either function: first derivative and two evaluations **OR** all three derivatives **OR** all four evaluations	$\bullet^1$ $f(x) = \sin 3x$ $f(0) = 0$ $f'(x) = 3\cos 3x$ $f'(0) = 3$ $f''(x) = -9\sin 3x$ $f''(0) = 0$ $f'''(x) = -27\cos 3x$ $f'''(0) = -27$ $f(x) = f(0) + f'(0)x + \dfrac{f''(0)}{2!}x^2 + \dfrac{f'''(0)}{3!}x^3 \ldots$	
	$\bullet^2$ complete derivatives and evaluations **AND** substitute	$\bullet^2$ $f(x) = 3x - \dfrac{27}{3!}x^3$ $= 3x - \dfrac{9}{2}x^3$	
	$\bullet^3$ for second function: first derivative and two evaluations **OR** all three derivatives **OR** all four evaluations	$\bullet^3$ $f(x) = e^{4x}$ $f(0) = 1$ $f'(x) = 4e^{4x}$ $f'(0) = 4$ $f''(x) = 16e^{4x}$ $f''(0) = 16$ $f'''(x) = 64e^{4x}$ $f'''(0) = 64$	
	$\bullet^4$ complete derivatives and evaluations **AND** substitute	$\bullet^4$ $f(x) = 1 + 4x + \dfrac{16x^2}{2} + \dfrac{64x^3}{6}$ $= 1 + 4x + 8x^2 + \dfrac{32}{3}x^3$	
	$\bullet^5$ multiply expressions	$\bullet^5$ $e^{4x}\sin 3x = \left(3x - \dfrac{9}{2}x^3 \ldots\right)\left(1 + 4x + 8x^2 + \dfrac{32}{3}x^3 \ldots\right)$ $= 24x^3 - \dfrac{9}{2}x^3 + 12x^2 + 3x \ldots$	
	$\bullet^6$ multiply out and simplify[Note 2]	$\bullet^6$ $= 3x + 12x^2 + \dfrac{39}{2}x^3 \ldots$	

Notes:

1. If a candidate chooses to use the product rule to obtain the Maclaurin series for $e^{4x}\sin 3x$ without first obtaining series for e^{4x} and $\sin 3x$ separately then only $\bullet^5$ and $\bullet^6$ are potentially available. In this instance for the award of $\bullet^5$ apply the same principle as that used to award $\bullet^1$ and $\bullet^3$.

$f(x) = e^{4x}\sin 3x$ $f(0) = 0$

$f'(x) = 4e^{4x}\sin 3x + 3e^{4x}\cos 3x$ $f'(0) = 3$

$f''(x) = 7e^{4x}\sin 3x + 24e^{4x}\cos 3x$ $f''(0) = 24$

$f'''(x) = -44e^{4x}\sin 3x + 117e^{4x}\cos 3x$ $f'''(0) = 117$

2. At $\bullet^6$ the appearance of terms in x^4 or above should be disregarded.

Question	Generic scheme	Illustrative scheme	Max mark
6.	**Method 2**		6
	•^{1} state the Maclaurin expansion for $\sin x$ [1]	•^{1} $\sin x = x - \dfrac{x^3}{3!}\ldots$	
	•^{2} substitute	•^{2} $\sin 3x = 3x - \dfrac{(3x)^3}{3!}\ldots$ $$\sin 3x = 3x - \dfrac{9x^3}{2}\ldots$$	
	•^{3} state the Maclaurin expansion for e^x [1]	•^{3} $e^x = 1 + x + \dfrac{x^2}{2!} + \dfrac{x^3}{3!}\ldots$	
	•^{4} substitute	•^{4} $e^{4x} = 1 + 4x + \dfrac{(4x)^2}{2!} + \dfrac{(4x)^3}{3!}\ldots$ $$e^{4x} = 1 + 4x + 8x^2 + \dfrac{32x^3}{3}\ldots$$	
	•^{5} multiply expressions	•^{5} $e^{4x}\sin 3x = (1 + 4x + 8x^2\ldots)\left(3x - \dfrac{9x^3}{2}\ldots\right)$	
	•^{6} multiply out and simplify	•^{6} $e^{4x}\sin 3x = 3x + 12x^2 + \dfrac{39x^3}{2} + \ldots.$	

Notes:
1. For a candidate who writes down $\sin 3x = 3x - \dfrac{(3x)^3}{3!}\ldots$ without first writing down the series for $\sin x$ then •^{1} may be awarded. A similar principle may be applied to the awarding of •^{3} if required.
2. At •^{6} the appearance of terms in x^4 or above should be disregarded.

7.	(a)		•^{1} calculate determinant [1]	•^{1} -2	1

Notes:
1. If a candidate chooses to find A^{-1} then •^{1} is only available where '$\det A$' is clearly identified.

Question	Generic scheme	Illustrative scheme	Max mark
7. (b)	**Method 1**		3
	$\bullet^2$ find A^2	$\bullet^2$ $A^2 = \begin{pmatrix} 4 & 0 \\ \lambda & 1 \end{pmatrix}$	
	$\bullet^3$ use an appropriate method	$\bullet^3$ $A^2 = \begin{pmatrix} 2 & 0 \\ \lambda & -1 \end{pmatrix} + \begin{pmatrix} 2 & 0 \\ 0 & 2 \end{pmatrix}$ $A^2 = A + 2I$	
	$\bullet^4$ write in required form and explicitly state values of p and q Note 1	$\bullet^4$ $p = 1$ **and** $q = 2$	
	Method 2		
	$\bullet^2$ find A^2	$\bullet^2$ $A^2 = \begin{pmatrix} 4 & 0 \\ \lambda & 1 \end{pmatrix}$	
	$\bullet^3$ use an appropriate method	$\bullet^3$ $A^2 = p\begin{pmatrix} 2 & 0 \\ \lambda & -1 \end{pmatrix} + q\begin{pmatrix} 1 & 0 \\ 0 & 1 \end{pmatrix}$	
	$\bullet^4$ write in required form and explicitly state values of p and q Note 1	$\bullet^4$ $A^2 = A + 2I$ $p = 1$ **and** $q = 2$	

Notes:

1. $\begin{pmatrix} 4 & 0 \\ \lambda & 1 \end{pmatrix} = \begin{pmatrix} 2 & 0 \\ \lambda & -1 \end{pmatrix} + 2\begin{pmatrix} 1 & 0 \\ 0 & 1 \end{pmatrix}$ is acceptable for $\bullet^4$ provided the values of p and q are explicitly stated.

Question	Generic scheme	Illustrative scheme	Max mark
(c)	$\bullet^5$ square expression found in (b)[1,2,3]	$\bullet^5$ $A^4 = (A + 2I)^2$ $\quad = A^2 + 4AI + 4I^2$ $\quad = A + 2I + 4A + 4I$	2
	$\bullet^6$ substitute for A^2 and complete process	$\bullet^6$ $\quad = 5A + 6I$	

Notes:

1. $\bullet^5$ may be obtained by squaring $\begin{pmatrix} 4 & 0 \\ \lambda & 1 \end{pmatrix}$ to give $\begin{pmatrix} 16 & 0 \\ 5\lambda & 1 \end{pmatrix}$ and identifying the coefficient of A as 5. This leads to $\bullet^6$ using the same method as in (b).
2. Accept equivalent expressions e.g. $= A^2 + 4A + 4I$.
3. Candidates may calculate A^3 first so $\bullet^5$ can be awarded for $A^3 = 3A + 2I$.

Question	Generic scheme	Illustrative scheme	Max mark
8. (a)	$\bullet^1$ correctly plot z on Argand diagram[1,2,3,4]	$\bullet^1$	1

Notes:
1. Do not penalise the omission of the diagonal line.
2. Treat alternative axis labels as bad form (to include the case where there are no labels).
3. Accept a point labelled using coordinates: $\left(\sqrt{3},-1\right)$ and, in this instance, $\left(\sqrt{3},-i\right)$.
4. The minimum acceptable response for the award of $\bullet^1$ is a point in quadrant 4 together with $\sqrt{3}$ and -1 (or $-i$).

(b)	$\bullet^2$ find modulus or argument[1,2,3,6]	$\bullet^2$ $\left\vert w\right\vert = 2a$ or $\arg(w)=-\dfrac{\pi}{6}$	2
	$\bullet^3$ complete and express in polar form[3,4,5,6]	$\bullet^3$ $w = 2a\left(\cos\left(-\dfrac{\pi}{6}\right)+i\sin\left(-\dfrac{\pi}{6}\right)\right)$	

Notes:
1. For the award of $\bullet^2$ and $\bullet^3$ accept any answer of the form $-\dfrac{\pi}{6}+2k\pi$, $k \in \mathbb{Z}$.

2. For the award of $\bullet^2$ and $\bullet^3$ accept any answer of the form $(-30+360k)°$, $k \in \mathbb{Z}$.
3. A candidate who chooses to work in degrees can only be awarded $\bullet^3$ provided the degree symbol appears at some point within question 8.
4. Award $\bullet^3$ for $w = 2a\left(\cos\left(\dfrac{\pi}{6}\right)-i\sin\left(\dfrac{\pi}{6}\right)\right)$.

5. At $\bullet^3$ do not accept $w = a\left[2\left(\cos\left(-\dfrac{\pi}{6}\right)+i\sin\left(-\dfrac{\pi}{6}\right)\right)\right]$.

6. Working subsequent to the appearance of $-\dfrac{\pi}{6}$ should be penalised where it leads to the use of an incorrect argument.

Question	Generic scheme	Illustrative scheme	Max mark
8. (c)	**Method 1**		3
	$\bullet^4$ process modulus	$\bullet^4$ $256a^8$	
	$\bullet^5$ process argument[1,2,3,4,5]	$\bullet^5$ $...\left(\cos\left(-\dfrac{8\pi}{6}\right) + i\sin\left(-\dfrac{8\pi}{6}\right)\right)$	
	$\bullet^6$ evaluate and express in form $ka^n\left(x + i\sqrt{y}\right)$	$\bullet^6$ $w^8 = 128a^8\left(-1 + i\sqrt{3}\right)$	

Notes:

1. For the award of $\bullet^5$ accept any answer of the form $-\dfrac{4\pi}{3} + 2k\pi$, $k \in \mathbb{Z}$.

2. For the award of $\bullet^5$ accept any answer of the form $(-240 + 360k)°$, $k \in \mathbb{Z}$.

3. A candidate who chooses to work in degrees can only be awarded $\bullet^5$ provided the degree symbol appears at some point within question 8.

4. Do not penalise unsimplified fractions.

5. Award $\bullet^5$ for $...\left(\cos\dfrac{8\pi}{6} - i\sin\dfrac{8\pi}{6}\right)$.

Question	Generic scheme	Illustrative scheme	Max mark
	Method 2		3
	$\bullet^4$ find w^2 correctly and attempt to find a higher power of w [Note 1]	$\bullet^4$ e.g. $w^2 = a^2\left(2 - 2i\sqrt{3}\right)$ and $w^3 = a^2\left(2 - 2i\sqrt{3}\right) \times a\left(\sqrt{3} - i\right)$	
	$\bullet^5$ obtain w^4	$\bullet^5$ $w^4 = a^4\left(-8 - 8i\sqrt{3}\right)$	
	$\bullet^6$ complete expansion and express in form $ka^n\left(x + i\sqrt{y}\right)$	$\bullet^6$ $w^8 = 128a^8\left(-1 + i\sqrt{3}\right)$	

Notes:

1. Accept the omission of 'a' at $\bullet^4$ and $\bullet^5$ provided a^8 appears in the final answer.

Question	Generic scheme	Illustrative scheme	Max mark
	Method 3		3
	$\bullet^4$ write down full binomial expansion[1,2]	$\bullet^4$ $\begin{pmatrix}8\\0\end{pmatrix}\left(\sqrt{3}\right)^8(-i)^0 + \begin{pmatrix}8\\1\end{pmatrix}\left(\sqrt{3}\right)^7(-i)^1$ $+ \begin{pmatrix}8\\2\end{pmatrix}\left(\sqrt{3}\right)^7(-i)^2 ... + \begin{pmatrix}8\\8\end{pmatrix}\left(\sqrt{3}\right)^0(-i)^8$	
	$\bullet^5$ simplifies individual terms	$\bullet^5$ $81 - 216i\sqrt{3} - 756 + 504i\sqrt{3}$ $+ 630 - 168i\sqrt{3} - 84 + 8i\sqrt{3} + 1$	
	$\bullet^6$ complete expansion and express in form $ka^n\left(x + i\sqrt{y}\right)$	$\bullet^6$ $w^8 = 128a^8\left(-1 + i\sqrt{3}\right)$	

Notes:

1. For the award of $\bullet^4$ a **full** expansion must be written out.

2. Accept the omission of 'a' at $\bullet^4$ and $\bullet^5$ provided a^8 appears in the final answer.

Question	Generic scheme	Illustrative scheme	Max mark
9.	•[1] know to use integration by parts AND start process[1,2,3]	•[1] $\frac{1}{8}x^8(\ln x)^2 - \ldots$	6
	•[2] correct choice of functions to differentiate and integrate AND application thereof [1,2,3]	•[2] $\ldots - \frac{1}{8}\int x^8 \times \frac{d}{dx}((\ln x)^2)\,dx$	
	•[3] differentiate $(\ln x)^2$ [4]	•[3] $\frac{1}{8}x^8(\ln x)^2 - \frac{1}{4}\int x^7(\ln x)\,dx$	
	•[4] know to use second application and begin process[1,2,3,4]	•[4] $\ldots - \left[\frac{1}{32}x^8(\ln x) - \frac{1}{32}\int x^8\left(\frac{1}{x}\right)dx\right]$	
	•[5] complete second application	•[5] $\ldots - \left[\frac{1}{32}x^8(\ln x) - \frac{1}{256}x^8\right]$	
	•[6] simplify[5]	•[6] $\frac{1}{8}x^8(\ln x)^2 - \frac{1}{32}x^8(\ln x) + \frac{1}{256}x^8 + c$	

Notes:
1. For candidates who attempt to integrate $(\ln x)^2$ and differentiate x^7 then •[1], •[4] and •[6] may be awarded but not •[2], •[3] and •[5].
2. Evidence of use of integration by parts would be the appearance of an attempt to integrate one term and differentiate the other.
3. For candidates who attempt to substitute for $\ln x$ e.g. $t = \ln x$ leading to $\int t^2 e^{8t}\,dt$ then

   •[1] becomes available upon evidence of using integration by parts ie. $t^2 \cdot \frac{1}{8}e^{8t} - \ldots$

   •[6] is only available for a final answer expressed as a function of x.

4. For candidates who incorrectly differentiate $(\ln x)^2$ and do not require a second application of integration by parts, only •[1], •[2] and •[6] are available.
5. Do not penalise the omission of "$+c$".

Question	Generic scheme	Illustrative scheme	Max mark
10.	•[1] give counterexample	•[1] e.g. choose $p = 7$ **COUNTEREXAMPLE** $2(7) + 1 = 15$ and since $15 = 5 \times 3$, hence not prime, statement is false.	4
	PROOF	**PROOF**	
	•[2] set up n [Notes 1,2]	•[2] $n = 3a + 1, \ a \in \mathbb{N}_0$	
	•[3] consider expansion of n^3 [Note 3]	•[3] $n^3 = 27a^3 + 27a^2 + 9a + 1$	
	•[4] complete proof with conclusion[4]	•[4] $= 3(9a^3 + 9a^2 + 3a) + 1$ and statement such as "so n^3 has remainder 1 when divided by 3 $\therefore$ statement is true".	

Notes:
1. Do not penalise the omission of $a \in \mathbb{N}_0$ in •[2].
2. Treat a statement such as $n = 3n + 1$ as bad form.
3. •[3] can only be awarded for the correct expansion of $(3a + 1)^3$.
4. Minimum statement of conclusion in •[4] is "true".
5. Where a candidate invokes an incorrect use of proof by contradiction full credit may still be available provided all relevant steps are included.

Question			Generic scheme	Illustrative scheme	Max mark
11.			**Method 1**		4
			$\bullet^1$ state differential equation[1,2]	$\bullet^1$ $\dfrac{dh}{dt}=5$	
			$\bullet^2$ state relationship or apply chain rule[3]	$\bullet^2$ $\dfrac{dV}{dt}=\dfrac{dV}{dh}\cdot\dfrac{dh}{dt}$ $V=h^3$	
			$\bullet^3$ find the rate of change of volume with respect to height[3]	$\bullet^3$ $\dfrac{dV}{dh}=3h^2$	
			$\bullet^4$ evaluate[4]	$\bullet^4$ $\dfrac{dV}{dt}=3h^2\times5=3(3)^2\times5=135\ \text{cm}^3\,\text{s}^{-1}$	
			Method 2		
			$\bullet^1$ express volume as a function of time	$\bullet^1$ $V=125t^3$	
			$\bullet^2$ find rate of change of volume with respect to time	$\bullet^2$ $\dfrac{dV}{dt}=375t^2$	
			$\bullet^3$ find value of t	$\bullet^3$ $t=\dfrac{3}{5}$	
			$\bullet^4$ evaluate	$\bullet^4$ $\dfrac{dV}{dt}=375\left(\dfrac{3}{5}\right)^2=135\ \text{cm}^3\,\text{s}^{-1}$	

Notes:
1. A candidate who assumes that only the height changes — and that the length and breadth are constant — can be awarded $\bullet^1$ and $\bullet^2$ only.
2. Where a candidate uses the wrong formula for the volume of a cube only $\bullet^1$ and $\bullet^2$ are available.
3. A candidate using Method 1 who writes $\dfrac{dV}{dt}=3h^2\dfrac{dh}{dt}$ can be awarded $\bullet^2$ and $\bullet^3$.
4. To award $\bullet^4$ there must be evidence of substituting 3 and 5. Correct units must also be included.

Question	Generic scheme	Illustrative scheme	Max mark
12. (a)	•^{1} correct shape •^{2} graph passes through $2c$ on the positive x- and y-axes	•^{1,2} 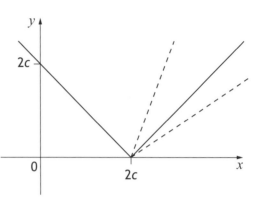	2

Notes:

1. To award •^{2}, the second arm must be sketched to within $15°$ of the reflected angle.

(b)	•^{3} graph of $y=\left|2f(x)\right|$ passing through $2c$ on the positive y-axis [1] •^{4} correct shape (symmetrical V) meeting positive x-axis at c[2]	•^{3,4}	2

Notes:
1. For a candidate who sketches the graph of $y=2f(x)$ award •^{3} for showing a straight line passing through $(0,-2c)$.
2. To award •^{4}, the second arm must be sketched to within $15°$ of the reflected angle.

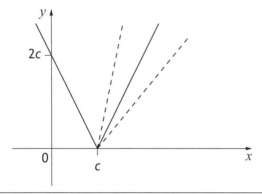

Question	Generic scheme	Illustrative scheme	Max mark
13.	$\bullet^1$ correct application of partial fractions	$\bullet^1$ $\dfrac{3x+32}{(x+4)(6-x)} = \dfrac{A}{x+4} + \dfrac{B}{6-x}$	9
	$\bullet^2$ start process	$\bullet^2$ $3x+32 = A(6-x) + B(x+4)$	
	$\bullet^3$ calculate one value	$\bullet^3$ $A = 2$	
	$\bullet^4$ calculate second value	$\bullet^4$ $B = 5$	
	$\bullet^5$ re-state integral in partial fractions	$\bullet^5$ $\displaystyle\int_{3}^{4}\left(\dfrac{2}{(x+4)} + \dfrac{5}{(6-x)}\right)dx$	
	$\bullet^6$ one term correctly integrated [1]	$\bullet^6$ $\left[2\ln\lvert x+4\rvert \dots\right.$	
	$\bullet^7$ integrate second term correctly [1]	$\bullet^7$ $\left.\dots -5\ln\lvert 6-x\rvert\right]_{3}^{4}$	
	$\bullet^8$ substitute limits	$\bullet^8$ $\left(2\ln\lvert 4+4\rvert - 5\ln\lvert 6-4\rvert\right)$ $-\left(2\ln\lvert 3+4\rvert - 5\ln\lvert 6-3\rvert\right)$	
	$\bullet^9$ evaluate to expected form[Note 3]	$\bullet^9$ $= \ln\dfrac{486}{49}$	

Notes:
1. Do not penalise lack of modulus signs unless the candidate attempts to integrate $\dfrac{1}{x-6}$ rather than $\dfrac{1}{6-x}$.
2. Award maximum [8/9] for appropriate working leading to $\ln\dfrac{98}{243}$ ($\bullet^9$ lost) or $\ln\dfrac{2048}{11907}$ ($\bullet^7$ lost).
3. Do not penalise unsimplified fractions in $\bullet^9$.

Question	Generic scheme	Illustrative scheme	Max mark
14. (a)	$\bullet^1$ convert any two components of L_2 to parametric form [1]	$\bullet^1$ two from $x = 3-2\mu$, $y = 8+\mu$, $z = -1+3\mu$	5
	$\bullet^2$ two linear equations involving two distinct parameters	$\bullet^2$ two from $4+3\lambda = 3-2\mu$, $2+4\lambda = 8+\mu$, $-7\lambda = -1+3\mu$	
	$\bullet^3$ find parameter values	$\bullet^3$ $\lambda = 1$, $\mu = -2$	
	$\bullet^4$ verify third component in **both** equations or equivalent	$\bullet^4$ e.g. $z_1 = -7\times 1$ and $z_2 = 3(-2)-1$ therefore the lines intersect.	
	$\bullet^5$ find point of intersection	$\bullet^5$ $(7, 6, -7)$	

Notes:
1. A candidate who uses λ as the second parameter can only be awarded $\bullet^1$ unless this is rectified later in the question.
2. Do not penalise the omission of the statement 'therefore the lines intersect'.

Question	Generic scheme	Illustrative scheme	Max mark
14. (b)	•[6] identify first direction vector [1,2,3]	•[6] $\mathbf{d}_1 = 3\mathbf{i} + 4\mathbf{j} - 7\mathbf{k}$	4
	•[7] identify second direction vector [1,2,3]	•[7] $\mathbf{d}_2 = -2\mathbf{i} + \mathbf{j} + 3\mathbf{k}$	
	•[8] calculate magnitudes and scalar product	•[8] $|\mathbf{d}_1| = \sqrt{74}$, $|\mathbf{d}_2| = \sqrt{14}$ and $\mathbf{d}_1 \cdot \mathbf{d}_2 = -6 + 4 - 21 = -23$	
	•[9] calculate obtuse angle [4,5]	•[9] $\cos^{-1}\left(\dfrac{-23}{\sqrt{74}\sqrt{14}}\right) \approx 135 \cdot 6°$	

Notes:
1. For $L_1 = 3\mathbf{i} + 4\mathbf{j} - 7\mathbf{k}$ and $L_2 = -2\mathbf{i} + \mathbf{j} + 3\mathbf{k}$ or equivalent, lose •[6] but •[7] is available (repeated error).
2. Do not penalise $\mathbf{L}_1 = 3\mathbf{i} + 4\mathbf{j} - 7\mathbf{k}$ and $\mathbf{L}_2 = -2\mathbf{i} + \mathbf{j} + 3\mathbf{k}$.
3. For $L_1 : 3\mathbf{i} + 4\mathbf{j} - 7\mathbf{k}$ and $L_2 : -2\mathbf{i} + \mathbf{j} + 3\mathbf{k}$ or equivalent, •[6] and •[7] are both available.
4. For the award of •[9] accept 136°.
5. •[9] is not available to candidates who calculate an obtuse angle correctly but who subsequently calculate an acute angle.

Question	Generic scheme	Illustrative scheme	Max mark
15.	•[1] state auxiliary equation[1]	•[1] $m^2 + 5m + 6 = 0$ $m = -3$, $m = -2$	10
	•[2] solve auxiliary equation and state complementary function[2,3]	•[2] $y = Ae^{-3x} + Be^{-2x}$	
	•[3] construct particular integral	•[3] $y = Cx^2 + Dx + E$	
	•[4] differentiate particular integral	•[4] $\dfrac{dy}{dx} = 2Cx + D$ and $\dfrac{d^2y}{dx^2} = 2C$	
	•[5] calculate one coefficient of the particular integral	•[5] $C = 2$	
	•[6] calculate remaining coefficients	•[6] $D = -3, E = 1$ $y = Ae^{-3x} + Be^{-2x} + 2x^2 - 3x + 1$	
	•[7] differentiate general solution[3]	•[7] $\dfrac{dy}{dx} = -3Ae^{-3x} - 2Be^{-2x} + 4x - 3$	
	•[8] construct equations using given conditions	•[8] $A + B = -7$ and $3A + 2B = -6$ or equivalent	
	•[9] find one coefficient	•[9] $A = 8$ or $B = -15$	
	•[10] find other coefficient **AND** state particular solution	•[10] $y = 8e^{-3x} - 15e^{-2x} + 2x^2 - 3x + 1$	

Notes:
1. For •[1] do not penalise the omission of '= 0'.
2. •[2] can be awarded if the Complementary Function appears later as part of the general solution, as opposed to being explicitly stated immediately after solving the Auxiliary Equation.
3. A candidate who obtains $m = 2$ and $m = 3$ from a correct auxiliary equation, leading to $y = 20e^{3x} - 27e^{2x} + 2x^2 - 3x + 1$, cannot gain •[2] but all other marks are available.
4. Where a candidate substitutes the given conditions into the Complementary Function to obtain values of A and B and then finds the particular integral correctly •[8] and •[9] are unavailable.

Question			Generic scheme	Illustrative scheme	Max mark
16.			**Method 1** — working in minutes ($t = 0$ at noon)		9
			$\bullet^1$ construct integral equation Note 1	$\bullet^1$ $\displaystyle\int \frac{1}{(T-T_F)}\,dT = \int -k\,dt$	
			$\bullet^2$ integrate [2]	$\bullet^2$ $\ln(T-T_F) = -kt + c$	
			$\bullet^3$ find constant, c	$\bullet^3$ $\ln(9\cdot 8 - 4) = -k(0) + c$ $c = \ln 5\cdot 8$	
			$\bullet^4$ substitute using given information [4]	$\bullet^4$ $\ln(6\cdot 5 - 4) = -15k + \ln 5\cdot 8$	
			$\bullet^5$ find constant, k	$\bullet^5$ $k = \dfrac{\ln 2\cdot 5 - \ln 5\cdot 8}{-15} = 0\cdot 05610\ldots$	
			$\bullet^6$ substitute given condition	$\bullet^6$ $\ln(25 - 4) = -0\cdot 05610\ldots t + \ln 5\cdot 8$	
			$\bullet^7$ know how to find time	$\bullet^7$ $t = \dfrac{\ln 21 - \ln 5\cdot 8}{-0\cdot 05610\ldots}$	
			$\bullet^8$ calculate time	$\bullet^8$ $t = -22\cdot 93\ldots$	
			$\bullet^9$ state the time to the nearest minute [3]	$\bullet^9$ The liquid was placed in the fridge at 11:37 (am).	
			Method 2 — working in minutes ($t = 0$ when $T = 25$)		
			$\bullet^1$ construct integral equation Note 1	$\bullet^1$ $\displaystyle\int \frac{1}{(T-T_F)}\,dT = \int -k\,dt$	
			$\bullet^2$ integrate [2]	$\bullet^2$ $\ln(T-T_F) = -kt + c$	
			$\bullet^3$ find constant, c.	$\bullet^3$ $\ln(25 - 4) = -k(0) + c$, $c = \ln 21$	
			$\bullet^4$ substitute using given information	$\bullet^4$ $\ln(9\cdot 8 - 4) = -k(t) + \ln 21$	
			$\bullet^5$ know to use $t + 15$ Note 5	$\bullet^5$ appearance of $(t+15)$	
			$\bullet^6$ use given condition	$\bullet^6$ $\ln(6\cdot 5 - 4) = -k(t+15) + \ln 21$	
			$\bullet^7$ find constant, k Note 6	$\bullet^7$ $k = -\dfrac{1}{15}\ln\left(\dfrac{2\cdot 5}{5\cdot 8}\right) = 0\cdot 05610\ldots$	
			$\bullet^8$ calculate time	$\bullet^8$ $t = \ln\left(\dfrac{21}{5\cdot 8}\right) \div 0\cdot 05610\ldots = 22\cdot 93$	
			$\bullet^9$ state the time to the nearest minute [3]	$\bullet^9$ The liquid was placed in the fridge at 11:37 (am).	

Question			Generic scheme	Illustrative scheme	Max mark
16.			**Method 3** — working in hours ($t = 0$ at midnight)		9
			•[1] construct integral equation [Note 1]	•[1] $\int \dfrac{1}{(T - T_F)}\, dT = \int -k\, dt$	
			•[2] integrate [2]	•[2] $\ln(T - T_F) = -kt + c$	
			•[3] use initial conditions	•[3] $\ln 5 \cdot 8 = -12k + c$	
			•[4] interpret later time	•[4] $\ln 2 \cdot 5 = -12 \cdot 25k + c$	
			•[5] find constant, k	•[5] $\ln 5 \cdot 8 - \ln 2 \cdot 5 = 0 \cdot 25k$ $$k = 3 \cdot 366..$$	
			•[6] find the constant, c	•[6] $\ln(9 \cdot 8 - 4) = -3 \cdot 366... \times 12 + c$ $$c = 42 \cdot 15..$$	
			•[7] know to find time	•[7] $\ln(25 - 4) = -3 \cdot 366...t + 42 \cdot 15$	
			•[8] calculate time	•[8] $t = \dfrac{42 \cdot 15 - \ln 21}{3 \cdot 366...}$ $$= 11 \cdot 62..$$	
			•[9] state the time to the nearest minute [3]	•[9] The liquid was placed in the fridge at 11:37 (am).	
			Method 4 — working in minutes ($t = 0$ when $T = 25$)		
			•[1] construct integral equation [Note 1]	•[1] $\int \dfrac{1}{(T - T_F)}\, dT = \int -k\, dt$	
			•[2] integrate [2]	•[2] $\ln(T - T_F) = -kt + c$ $T - T_F = e^{-kt+c}$ $T = Ae^{-kt} + T_F$ $T = Ae^{-kt} + 4$	
			•[3] use initial condition to calculate A	•[3] $25 = Ae^{-k(0)} + 4 \therefore A = 21$	
			•[4] substitute using given information	•[4] $9 \cdot 8 = 21e^{-kt} + 4$	
			•[5] know to use $t + 15$ [Note 7]	•[5] Appearance of $(t + 15)$.	
			•[6] substitute using given information	•[6] $6 \cdot 5 = 21e^{-k(t+15)} + 4$	
			•[7] find constant, k	•[7] $k = \dfrac{\ln\left(\dfrac{5 \cdot 8}{21}\right) - \ln\left(\dfrac{2 \cdot 5}{21}\right)}{15} = 0 \cdot 0561...$	
			•[8] calculate time	•[8] $t = \ln\left(\dfrac{21}{5 \cdot 8}\right) \div 0 \cdot 05610... = 22 \cdot 93...$	
			•[9] state the time to the nearest minute [3]	•[9] The liquid was placed in the fridge at 11:37 (am).	

Question	Generic scheme	Illustrative scheme	Max mark

Notes:

General note:

Many candidates may use a combination of the given methods. For all methods the evidence for $\bullet^1$, $\bullet^2$, $\bullet^8$ and $\bullet^9$ is the same. To award $\bullet^3$ up to $\bullet^7$ note that:

    two marks are awarded for using two different values of T

    one mark is awarded for finding the constant of integration

    one mark is awarded for finding or eliminating k (refer to Note **6**)

    one mark is awarded for dealing with the elapsed time (noon until 12:15)

1. Do not penalise the omission of integral symbols at $\bullet^1$. (All Methods)
2. Do not penalise omission of "$+c$" at $\bullet^2$. However, it is necessary to access some later marks. (All Methods)
3. Where a candidate obtains an incorrect final answer because of earlier rounding, only $\bullet^9$ is unavailable. (All Methods)
4. For Method 1, if the candidate works in hours:

    $\bullet^4$ $\ln(6 \cdot 5 - 4) = -0 \cdot 25k + \ln(5 \cdot 8)$

    $\bullet^5$ $k = -4(\ln 2 \cdot 5 - \ln 5 \cdot 8) = 3 \cdot 366...$

    $\bullet^6$ $\ln(25 - 4) = -3 \cdot 366...t + \ln 5 \cdot 8$

    $\bullet^7$ $t = \dfrac{\ln 21 - \ln 5 \cdot 8}{-3 \cdot 366...}$

    $\bullet^8$ $t = -0 \cdot 3822..$

5. For Method 2, if the candidate works in hours:

    $\bullet^5$ appearance of $(t + 0 \cdot 25)$

    $\bullet^6$ $\ln(6 \cdot 5 - 4) = -k(t + 0 \cdot 25) + \ln 21$

    $\bullet^7$ $k = -\dfrac{1}{0 \cdot 25}\ln\left(\dfrac{2 \cdot 5}{5 \cdot 8}\right) = 3 \cdot 366...$

    $\bullet^8$ $t = \ln\left(\dfrac{21}{5 \cdot 8}\right) \div 0 \cdot 366... = 0 \cdot 3822...$

6. In Method 2 $\bullet^7$ can be awarded for eliminating k.

7. For Method 4, if the candidate works in hours:

    $\bullet^5$ appearance of $(t + 0 \cdot 25)$

    $\bullet^6$ $6 \cdot 5 = 21e^{-k(t+0 \cdot 25)} + 4$

    $\bullet^7$ $k = \dfrac{\ln\left(\dfrac{5 \cdot 8}{21}\right) - \ln\left(\dfrac{2 \cdot 5}{21}\right)}{0 \cdot 25} = 3 \cdot 366...$

    $\bullet^8$ $t = \ln\left(\dfrac{21}{5 \cdot 8}\right) \div 3 \cdot 366... = 0 \cdot 3822...$

ADVANCED HIGHER MATHEMATICS
2017

Question	Generic scheme	Illustrative scheme	Max mark
1.	$\bullet^1$ write down binomial expansion [1,3,4]	$\bullet^1 \ = \begin{pmatrix} 3 \\ 0 \end{pmatrix}\left(\dfrac{2}{y^2}\right)^3 + \begin{pmatrix} 3 \\ 1 \end{pmatrix}\left(\dfrac{2}{y^2}\right)^2(-5y)$ $+ \begin{pmatrix} 3 \\ 2 \end{pmatrix}\left(\dfrac{2}{y^2}\right)(-5y)^2 + \begin{pmatrix} 3 \\ 3 \end{pmatrix}(-5y)^3$	4
	$\bullet^2$ resolve signs [3,4]		
	$\bullet^3$ simplify coefficients or powers of y [2,4]		
	$\bullet^4$ complete simplification and obtain expression [2,4,5,6]	$\bullet^{2,3,4} \quad \dfrac{8}{y^6} - \dfrac{60}{y^3} + 150 - 125y^3$	

Notes:
1. Accept any correct form for binomial coefficients.
2. Accept negative powers of y.
3. For candidates who expand $\left(\dfrac{2}{y^2} + 5y\right)^3$ using the Binomial Theorem $\bullet^1$ and $\bullet^2$ are not available.
4. Candidates who expand $\left(\dfrac{2}{y^2} - 5y\right)^3$ without using the Binomial Theorem may be awarded $\bullet^2$, $\bullet^3$ and $\bullet^4$ but $\bullet^1$ is not available.
5. $\bullet^4$ is not available for a final expression which contains the term "$150y^\circ$".
6. Do not award $\bullet^4$ where the candidate produces incorrect working subsequent to a correct simplification.

Question	Generic scheme	Illustrative scheme	Max mark
2.	$\bullet^1$ state expression	$\bullet^1 \ \dfrac{x^2 - 6x + 20}{(x+1)(x-2)^2} = \dfrac{A}{(x+1)} + \dfrac{B}{(x-2)} + \dfrac{C}{(x-2)^2}$	4
	$\bullet^2$ form equation	$\bullet^2 \ x^2 - 6x + 20 = A(x-2)^2 + B(x+1)(x-2) + C(x+1)$	
	$\bullet^3$ obtain two of A, B and C	$\bullet^3 \ A = 3, \ B = -2, \ C = 4$	
	$\bullet^4$ obtain final constant and state expression [1]	$\bullet^4 \ \dfrac{3}{(x+1)} - \dfrac{2}{(x-2)} + \dfrac{4}{(x-2)^2}$	

Notes:
1. At $\bullet^4$ accept $\dfrac{3}{(x+1)} + \dfrac{-2}{(x-2)} + \dfrac{4}{(x-2)^2}$ but do not accept $\dfrac{3}{(x+1)} + -\dfrac{2}{(x-2)} + \dfrac{4}{(x-2)^2}$.

Question	Generic scheme	Illustrative scheme	Max mark
3.	$\bullet^1$ evidence use of quotient rule with one term of numerator correct	$\bullet^1 \ 2xe^{x^2-1}(x^2-1) - \ldots$	3
	$\bullet^2$ complete differentiation	$\bullet^2 \ \dfrac{\ldots 2xe^{x^2-1}}{(x^2-1)^2}$	
	$\bullet^3$ simplify [1,2,3]	$\bullet^3 \ \dfrac{2xe^{x^2-1}(x^2-2)}{(x^2-1)^2}$	

Question			Generic scheme		Illustrative scheme	Max mark

Notes:

1. At $\bullet^3$ accept $\dfrac{2x^3 e^{x^2-1} - 4xe^{x^2-1}}{(x^2-1)^2}$ but not accept $\dfrac{2xe^{x^2-1}((x^2-1)-1)}{(x^2-1)^2}$ (GM Principle (l)).

2. Do not award $\bullet^3$ where the candidate produces further incorrect simplification subsequent to a correct answer.

3. Where a candidate differentiates incorrectly $\bullet^3$ may be available provided like terms are collected in the numerator. Where this is not possible the expression should be fully factorised (this need not extend to exponential functions of differing powers). Where no simplification is possible $\bullet^3$ is not available.

Question			Generic scheme		Illustrative scheme	Max mark
4.	(a)		$\bullet^1$ evidence use of valid strategy	$\bullet^1$	e.g. $a + 4d = -6$ $a + 11d = -34$	2
			$\bullet^2$ obtain values of a and d[1]	$\bullet^2$	$a = 10$, $d = -4$	

Notes:

1. Candidates who state correct values for both a and d without working may be awarded $\bullet^1$ and $\bullet^2$.

Question			Generic scheme		Illustrative scheme	Max mark
	(b)		$\bullet^3$ set up equation	$\bullet^3$	$\dfrac{n}{2}[20 - 4(n-1)] = -144$	3
			$\bullet^4$ rearrange to standard form[1]	$\bullet^4$	$2n^2 - 12n - 144 = 0$	
			$\bullet^5$ determine the value of n[2]	$\bullet^5$	$n > 0 \therefore n = 12$	

Notes:

1. $\bullet^4$ may be awarded only where a quadratic equation has been expressed in standard form.
2. $\bullet^5$ may be awarded only where an invalid solution for n has been discarded.

Question			Generic scheme		Illustrative scheme	Max mark
5.	(a)	(i)	$\bullet^1$ set up augmented matrix	$\bullet^1$	$\begin{pmatrix} 1 & 2 & -1 & -3 \\ 4 & -2 & 3 & 11 \\ 3 & 1 & 2\lambda & 8 \end{pmatrix}$	4
			$\bullet^2$ obtain two zeros[1]	$\bullet^2$	$\begin{pmatrix} 1 & 2 & -1 & -3 \\ 0 & -10 & 7 & 23 \\ 0 & -5 & 2\lambda+3 & 17 \end{pmatrix}$	
			$\bullet^3$ complete row operations[1]	$\bullet^3$	$\begin{pmatrix} 1 & 2 & -1 & -3 \\ 0 & -10 & 7 & 23 \\ 0 & 0 & 4\lambda-1 & 11 \end{pmatrix}$	
			$\bullet^4$ obtain expression for z [2,3]	$\bullet^4$	$z = \dfrac{11}{4\lambda-1}$	
		(ii)	$\bullet^5$ state value of λ	$\bullet^5$	$\lambda = \dfrac{1}{4}$	1
	(b)		$\bullet^6$ find solution [4]	$\bullet^6$	$z = -1$, $y = -3$, $x = 2$	1

Notes:

1. Only Gaussian Elimination (i.e. a systematic approach using EROs) is acceptable for the award of $\bullet^2$ and $\bullet^3$.

2. Do not accept an answer of $(4\lambda - 1)z = 11$ when awarding $\bullet^4$.

3. At $\bullet^4$ accept an unsimplified expression for z e.g. $z = \dfrac{5 \cdot 5}{2\lambda - \frac{1}{2}}$.

4. Where decimal approximations are used $\bullet^6$ is available only where candidates work to 3sf or better.

Question			Generic scheme	Illustrative scheme	Max mark
6.			•[1] differentiate $5x^2$	•[1] $\dfrac{du}{dx} = 10x$ or $du = 10x\,dx$	6
			•[2] find limits for u [3]	•[2] $u = 0,\ u = \dfrac{1}{2}$	
			•[3] replace '$x\,dx$' [1,2]	•[3] $\dfrac{1}{10}\int \ldots du$	
			•[4] obtain integrand [1,2]	•[4] $\dfrac{1}{10}\displaystyle\int_0^{\frac{1}{2}} \dfrac{1}{\sqrt{1-u^2}}\,du$	
			•[5] integrate [2,3,4,5]	•[5] $\dfrac{1}{10}\left[\sin^{-1}u\right]_0^{\frac{1}{2}}$	
			•[6] evaluate [2,6,7,8]	•[6] $\dfrac{\pi}{60}$	

Notes:

1. At •[3] and •[4] treat as bad form situations where candidates either omit limits or retain limits for x.
2. Where candidates attempt to integrate an expression containing both u and x, where x is either inside the integrand or erroneously taken outside as a constant, only •[1] and •[2] may be available.
3. Where candidates do not change limits but who produce working leading to $\dfrac{1}{10}\left[\sin^{-1}(5x^2)\right]_0^{\frac{1}{\sqrt{10}}}$, •[2] may be awarded.
4. Where candidates show no working but write down $\dfrac{1}{10}\left[\sin^{-1}(5x^2)\right]_0^{\frac{1}{\sqrt{10}}}$, •[1] is not available.
5. •[5] and •[6] are unavailable to candidates who having been awarded •[4] subsequently proceed to $\dfrac{1}{10}\left[\dfrac{(1-u^2)^{\frac{1}{2}}}{-\frac{1}{2} \times 2u}\right]$.
6. For candidates who integrate incorrectly, •[6] may be available provided division by zero does not occur.
7. For candidates who, upon integrating, obtain a trigonometric expression and then work in degrees •[6] is unavailable.
8. Disregard the appearance of a decimal approximation subsequent to a simplified exact value.

Question			Generic scheme	Illustrative scheme	Max mark
7.	(a)	(i)	•[1] determine value of x	•[1] $x = 8$	1
		(ii)	•[2] find inverse [1]	•[2] $P^{-1} = \dfrac{1}{2}\begin{pmatrix} -1 & -2 \\ 5 & 8 \end{pmatrix}$	1
		(iii)	•[3] state transpose	•[3] $Q' = \begin{pmatrix} 2 & 4 \\ -3 & y \end{pmatrix}$	2
			•[4] obtain product [2,3]	•[4] $P^{-1}Q' = \begin{pmatrix} 2 & -2-y \\ -7 & 10+4y \end{pmatrix}$	

Notes:

1. At •[2] accept $P^{-1} = \dfrac{1}{2}\begin{pmatrix} -1 & -2 \\ 5 & x \end{pmatrix}$.

2. For •[4] accept $P^{-1}Q' = \dfrac{1}{2}\begin{pmatrix} 4 & -4-2y \\ -14 & 20+8y \end{pmatrix}$ but not $P^{-1}Q' = \dfrac{1}{2}\begin{pmatrix} -2+6 & -4-2y \\ 10-24 & 20+8y \end{pmatrix}$.

3. •[4] may be awarded only where y is present.

Question			Generic scheme	Illustrative scheme	Max mark
7.	(b)		•[5] state condition for singularity [1,2]	•[5] $\det R = 0$ or one row is a multiple of the other	2
			•[6] obtain value for z^2	•[6] $z = 15$	

Notes:
1. $\det R = 0$ may be stated or implied in the working for •[6].
2. For an answer of $z = 15$ without justification, •[5] is not available.

Question			Generic scheme	Illustrative scheme	Max mark
8.			•[1] start process	•[1] $1595 = 1 \times 1218 + 377$ $1218 = 3 \times 377 + 87$	4
			•[2] obtain remainder of 29 [1]	•[2] $377 = 4 \times 87 + 29$ $87 = 3 \times 29 + 0$	
			•[3] express gcd in terms of 377 and 1218	•[3] $29 = 377 - 4(1218 - 3 \times 377)$	
			•[4] state values of a and b [2]	•[4] $a = 13, b = -17$	

Notes:
1. At •[2] the gcd does not need to be explicitly stated.
2. The minimum requirement for •[4] is $1595 \times 13 + 1218 \times (-17) = 29$.

Question			Generic scheme	Illustrative scheme	Max mark
9.			•[1] separate variables and write down integral equation [1,7]	•[1] $\displaystyle\int \frac{dy}{1 + y^2} = \int e^{2x}\, dx$	5
			•[2] integrate LHS [2]	•[2] $\tan^{-1} y$	
			•[3] integrate RHS [3]	•[3] $\dfrac{1}{2}e^{2x} + c$	
			•[4] evaluate constant of integration [2,3,4,5]	•[4] $c = \dfrac{\pi}{4} - \dfrac{1}{2}$	
			•[5] express y in terms of x [3,5,6]	•[5] $y = \tan\left(\dfrac{1}{2}e^{2x} + \dfrac{\pi}{4} - \dfrac{1}{2}\right)$	

Notes:
1. Do not withhold •[1] where dy and dx have been omitted.
2. For candidates who integrate the LHS and obtain a logarithmic expression, •[2] and •[4] are not available.
3. For candidates who omit a constant of integration, •[3] may be awarded but •[4] and •[5] are unavailable.
4. At •[4] accept a decimal value for the constant of integration correct to at least 3sf ($0 \cdot 285$).
5. For candidates who work in degrees, •[4] is unavailable but •[5] may be awarded.
6. At •[5] do not accept e.g. $y = \tan\left(\dfrac{1}{2}e^{2x}\right) + \dfrac{\pi}{4} - \dfrac{1}{2}$, $y = \tan\dfrac{1}{2}e^{2x} + \dfrac{\pi}{4} - \dfrac{1}{2}$.
7. Candidates who use either Integration by Parts or the Integrating Factor Method receive 0/5.

Question			Generic scheme	Illustrative scheme	Max mark
10.	(a)		•[1] substitute formulae	•[1] $\displaystyle\sum_{r=1}^{n}\left(r^2 + \frac{1}{3}r\right) = \frac{n(n+1)(2n+1)}{6} + \frac{1}{3}\left(\frac{n(n+1)}{2}\right)$ $= \dfrac{n(n+1)((2n+1)+1)}{6}$	2
			•[2] factorise fully [1]	•[2] $= \dfrac{n(n+1)^2}{3}$	

Question			Generic scheme	Illustrative scheme	Max mark

Notes:
1. At $\bullet^2$ do not accept $\dfrac{n(n+1)(n+1)}{3}$ or $\dfrac{2n(n+1)^2}{6}$.

Question			Generic scheme	Illustrative scheme	Max mark
10.	(b)		$\bullet^3$ substitute $2p$ and 9	$\bullet^3$ $\dfrac{2p(2p+1)^2}{3}$ and $\dfrac{9(9+1)^2}{3}$ $\dfrac{2p(2p+1)^2}{3} - \dfrac{9(9+1)^2}{3}$	2
			$\bullet^4$ obtain expression	$\bullet^4$ $= \dfrac{2p(2p+1)^2}{3} - 300$	
11.			**Method 1** $\bullet^1$ take logarithms of both sides and apply rule[1] $\bullet^2$ differentiate LHS $\bullet^3$ evidence use of product rule and one term correct[2] $\bullet^4$ complete differentiation[2] $\bullet^5$ write $\dfrac{dy}{dx}$ in terms of x	$\bullet^1$ $\ln y = (2x^3+1)\ln x$ $\bullet^2$ $\dfrac{1}{y}\dfrac{dy}{dx}$ $\bullet^3$ $6x^2 \ln x$ or $\dfrac{2x^3+1}{x}$ $\bullet^4$ $6x^2 \ln x + \dfrac{2x^3+1}{x}$ $\bullet^5$ $\dfrac{dy}{dx} = x^{2x^3+1}\left(6x^2 \ln x + \dfrac{2x^3+1}{x}\right)$	5

Notes:
1. Accept "log" in lieu of "ln".
2. For candidates who do not attempt to use the product rule, $\bullet^3$ and $\bullet^4$ are not available.

Question			Generic scheme	Illustrative scheme	Max mark
12.	(a)		$\bullet^1$ show half-turn symmetry and indicate $(1, 2)$ [1,2] $\bullet^2$ demonstrate graph approaching parallel asymptote through $(0, 3)$ [3,4]	$\bullet^{1,2}$	2

Notes:
1. To award $\bullet^1$ the candidate's graph should exhibit a smooth change in concavity at the origin.
2. Evidence of $(1, 2)$ may appear in (b).
3. At $\bullet^2$ accept $y = \dfrac{1}{2}x + 3$ in lieu of $(0, 3)$.
4. Where a candidate's graph diverges from the asymptote in quadrant 1, $\bullet^2$ is not available.
5. For Graph 1 in the Commonly Observed Responses $\bullet^1$, $\bullet^2$, $\bullet^3$ and $\bullet^4$ are not available.
6. For Graph 2 in the Commonly Observed Responses $\bullet^1$, $\bullet^2$ and $\bullet^3$ are not available but $\bullet^4$ may be available where a second asymptote appears in (b).

Question			Generic scheme	Illustrative scheme	Max mark
12.	(b)		$\bullet^3$ apply modulus function to graph obtained in (a)[1,4] $\bullet^4$ illustrate asymptotes meeting on the y-axis[1,2,3]	$\bullet^{3,4}$ 	2

Notes:
1. To receive any credit, a candidate's graph from (a) must have a section lying in quadrant 1.
2. $\bullet^4$ is still available where a candidate's graph diverges from the asymptotes.
3. At $\bullet^4$ disregard the application of the modulus function to asymptotes.
4. Showing the image points is not required at $\bullet^3$.

	(c)		**State the range of values of $f'(x)$ given that $f'(0) = 2$.**		
			$\bullet^5$ state range[1,2,3]	$\bullet^5$ $\dfrac{1}{2} < f'(x) \le 2$	1

Notes:
1. Do not accept $\dfrac{1}{2} \le f'(x) \le 2$ or $\dfrac{1}{2} < f'(x) < 2$.

2. Accept " $f'(x) > \dfrac{1}{2}$ and $f'(x) \le 2$ " but not " $f'(x) > \dfrac{1}{2}$ or $f'(x) \le 2$ ".

3. Accept " $f'(x)$ is greater than $\dfrac{1}{2}$ and $f'(x)$ is less than or equal to 2". Do not accept " $f'(x)$ is between $\dfrac{1}{2}$ and 2".

Question			Generic scheme	Illustrative scheme	Max mark
13.			$\bullet^1$ write down contrapositive statement[1,2,7,8] $\bullet^2$ write down appropriate form for n[3,4,7] $\bullet^3$ show n^2 is odd[5,6,7] $\bullet^4$ communicate	$\bullet^1$ The contrapositive of the original statement is: If n is odd then n^2 is odd. $\bullet^2$ $n = 2k + 1$, $k \in \mathbb{Z}$ $\bullet^3$ $n^2 = 2(2k^2 + 2k) + 1$ which is odd. $\bullet^4$ Contrapositive statement is true therefore original statement is true.	4

Question	Generic scheme	Illustrative scheme	Max mark

Notes:

1. A candidate who incorrectly states the contrapositive as n^2 is odd $\Rightarrow n$ is odd (or any other statement masquerading as the contrapositive) and subsequently demonstrates that when n is odd then n^2 is odd may be awarded $\bullet^3$ only.

2. The minimum requirement for $\bullet^1$ is a statement such as:
   n is odd $\Rightarrow n^2$ is odd
   n is odd then n^2 is odd
   n is odd is a sufficient condition for n^2 is odd
   n is odd only if n^2 is odd
   n^2 is odd when n is odd
   Do not accept "n is odd, n^2 is odd" or "n is odd when n^2 is odd".

3. At $\bullet^2$ $k \in \mathbb{Z}$ is not required. Accept the form $n = 2k \pm a$, where a is a specified odd number.

4. For candidates who proceed from:

e.g.	$n = 2n + 1$	$\bullet^2$ and $\bullet^4$ are not available
e.g.	$n = 2k$	$\bullet^2$, $\bullet^3$ and $\bullet^4$ are not available
e.g.	$n = k + 1$	$\bullet^2$, $\bullet^3$ and $\bullet^4$ are not available (n is not always odd)
e.g.	$n = 4k + 1$	$\bullet^2$ is not available (not all odd numbers covered by this form)

5. At $\bullet^3$ accept $n^2 = 4(\ldots) + 1$, $n^2 = 2k(\ldots) + 1$ or $n^2 = 4k(\ldots) + 1$.

6. At $\bullet^3$ candidates must state a conclusion e.g. "which is odd".

7. Candidates who carry out a proof by contradiction may be awarded $\bullet^2$ and $\bullet^3$ only.

8. Candidates who write $\neg Q \Rightarrow \neg P$ may be awarded $\bullet^1$ where they either identify P and Q or have written $P \Rightarrow Q$.

Question	Generic scheme	Illustrative scheme	Max mark
14.	$\bullet^1$ construct auxiliary equation [1,9]	$\bullet^1$ $m^2 - 6m + 9 = 0$	10
	$\bullet^2$ solve auxiliary equation and state CF [2,3,4,5,6,7,9]	$\bullet^2$ $y = Ae^{3x} + Bxe^{3x}$	
	$\bullet^3$ state PI	$\bullet^3$ $y = C\sin x + D\cos x$ $\dfrac{dy}{dx} = C\cos x - D\sin x$	
	$\bullet^4$ obtain first and second derivatives of PI	$\bullet^4$ $\dfrac{d^2 y}{dx^2} = -C\sin x - D\cos x$	
	$\bullet^5$ substitute	$\bullet^5$ $-C\sin x - D\cos x$ $-6(C\cos x - D\sin x)$ $+9(C\sin x + D\cos x) = 8\sin x + 19\cos x$	
	$\bullet^6$ derive equations	$\bullet^6$ $8C + 6D = 8$ $-6C + 8D = 19$	
	$\bullet^7$ obtain both constants of PI	$\bullet^7$ $C = -\dfrac{1}{2}, D = 2$	
	$\bullet^8$ differentiate general solution [5,6,7,9,10]	$\bullet^8$ $\dfrac{dy}{dx} = 3Ae^{3x} + Be^{3x} + 3Bxe^{3x} - \dfrac{1}{2}\cos x - 2\sin x$	
	$\bullet^9$ determine first constant of general solution [7,8,9]	$\bullet^9$ $A = 5$ or $B = -14$	
	$\bullet^{10}$ determine second constant and state particular solution [3,7,9,10]	$\bullet^{10}$ $y = 5e^{3x} - 14xe^{3x} - \dfrac{1}{2}\sin x + 2\cos x$	

Question	Generic scheme	Illustrative scheme	Max mark

Notes:
1. $\bullet^1$ is not available where ' $=0$ ' has been omitted.
2. $\bullet^2$ can be awarded if the Complementary Function appears later as part of the general solution, as opposed to being explicitly stated immediately after solving the Auxiliary Equation.
3. Do not penalise the omission of ' $y = \ldots$ ' provided it appears at $\bullet^{10}$.
4. For candidates who obtain a CF of $y = Ae^{-3x} + Bxe^{-3x}$ only $\bullet^2$ is not available. In this case the particular solution is $y = 5e^{-3x} + 16xe^{-3x} - \frac{1}{2}\sin x + 2\cos x$.
5. For candidates who obtain two real and distinct roots $\bullet^2$ and $\bullet^8$ are not available.
6. For candidates who obtain roots of the form $p \pm qi$: if $p = 0$ and $q \neq 1$ $\bullet^2$ and $\bullet^8$ are not available, otherwise only $\bullet^2$ is not available.
7. For candidates who obtain a CF of $y = Ae^{3x} + Be^{3x}$, $\bullet^2$, $\bullet^8$, $\bullet^9$ and $\bullet^{10}$ are not available.
8. Where a candidate substitutes the given conditions into the CF to obtain values of A and B and then finds the PI correctly, $\bullet^9$ is not available.
9. Where a candidate does not find a PI only $\bullet^1$, $\bullet^2$, $\bullet^8$, $\bullet^9$ and $\bullet^{10}$ are available.
10. Where an error in the differentiation of the general solution results in the value of B being unobtainable then $\bullet^{10}$ is not available.

Question	Generic scheme	Illustrative scheme	Max mark
15. (a)	$\bullet^1$ obtain direction vector [1,2,4] $\bullet^2$ state parametric equations [3,4,5]	$\bullet^1$ $\mathbf{d} = \begin{pmatrix} 2 \\ 6 \\ -1 \end{pmatrix}$ or multiple thereof. $\bullet^2$ $\begin{aligned} x &= 2\lambda + 7 \\ y &= 6\lambda + 8 \\ z &= -\lambda + 1 \end{aligned}$ or $\begin{aligned} x &= 2\lambda - 3 \\ y &= 6\lambda - 22 \\ z &= -\lambda + 6 \end{aligned}$ or equivalent.	2

Notes:
1. For candidates who express the equation in either symmetric or vector form $\bullet^1$ is available for evidence of a correct direction vector; $\bullet^2$ is unavailable unless parametric equations appear at (c).
2. Throughout the question accept horizontal vector notation e.g. $(2, 6, -1)$.
3. A correct answer with no working receives full marks.
4. For an incorrect answer containing the correct direction vector but with no working, $\bullet^1$ is available.
5. For an answer with an incorrect direction vector and no working neither $\bullet^1$ nor $\bullet^2$ are available.

Question			Generic scheme		Illustrative scheme	Max mark
15.	(b)		•³ identify vectors	•³	Any two from $\overrightarrow{PQ} = \begin{pmatrix} -1 \\ 1 \\ -2 \end{pmatrix}$, $\overrightarrow{PR} = \begin{pmatrix} -5 \\ 6 \\ -8 \end{pmatrix}$, $\overrightarrow{QR} = \begin{pmatrix} -4 \\ 5 \\ -6 \end{pmatrix}$ or equivalent.	4
			•⁴ evidence of strategy for finding normal [1]	•⁴	$\overrightarrow{PQ} \times \overrightarrow{PR} = \begin{vmatrix} \mathbf{i} & \mathbf{j} & \mathbf{k} \\ -1 & 1 & -2 \\ -5 & 6 & -8 \end{vmatrix}$ or equivalent	
			•⁵ calculate normal	•⁵	$\mathbf{n} = \begin{pmatrix} 4 \\ 2 \\ -1 \end{pmatrix}$	
			•⁶ obtain equation	•⁶	$4x + 2y - z = 1$	

Notes:
1. Do not award •⁴ where the position vectors of P, Q or R are used.

	(c)		•⁷ substitute into equation of plane	•⁷	$4(2\lambda + 7) + 2(6\lambda + 8) - (-\lambda + 1) = 1$	3
			•⁸ find λ	•⁸	$\lambda = -2$	
			•⁹ determine coordinates of H [1]	•⁹	H$(3, -4, 3)$	

Notes:
1. Do not accept a position vector at •⁹.

16.			•¹ state form of integral [1,2,3]	•¹	$V = \pi \int x^2 \, dy$ or $V = \pi \int \left(f(y) \right)^2 dy$	5
			•² rearrange and substitute for x^2	•²	$V = \pi \int \left(9 - \dfrac{9}{4} y^2 \right) dy$	
			•³ calculate limits to match variable [4]	•³	$\int_0^2 \ldots dy$ or $y = 0, y = 2$	
			•⁴ integrate	•⁴	$V = \pi \left[9y - \dfrac{3y^3}{4} \right]_0^2$	
			•⁵ evaluate [5,6]	•⁵	$V = 12\pi$ (cubic units)	

Notes:
1. dy must appear for •¹ to be awarded.
2. •¹ may be awarded at •².
3. For candidates who write $V = \pi \int x^2 \, dx$, $V = \pi \int y^2 \, dy$ or $V = \pi \int y^2 \, dx$ and proceed to:

   (a) $V = \pi \int \left(9 - \dfrac{9}{4} y^2 \right) dy$ full credit may still be available.

   (b) $V = \pi \int \left(4 - \dfrac{4}{9} x^2 \right) dx$ •², •³, •⁴ and •⁵ may still be available.

   (c) $\pi \left[\dfrac{x^3}{3} \right]$ or $\pi \left[\dfrac{y^3}{3} \right]$ only •³ is available.

4. •³ may be awarded at •⁴.
5. •⁵ is not available where a candidate's evaluation necessarily leads to a negative answer.
6. At •⁵ units are not required.

Question			Generic scheme	Illustrative scheme	Max mark
17.	(a)		$\bullet^1$ state second root	$\bullet^1$ $2-i$	1
	(b)		$\bullet^2$ obtain two linear actors	$\bullet^2$ $z-(2+i),\ z-(2-i)$	6
			$\bullet^3$ obtain quadratic factor	$\bullet^3$ z^2-4z+5	
			$\bullet^4$ set up algebraic division or equivalent	$\bullet^4$ $(z^2-4z+5)\ \overline{\big)\,z^4-6z^3+16z^2-22z+q}$	
			$\bullet^5$ complete algebraic division	$\bullet^5$ $\ \ \ \ \ z^2-2z+3$ $z^2-4z+5\ \overline{\big)\,z^4-6z^3+16z^2-22z+q}$ $z^4-4z^3+5z^2$ $-2z^3+11z^2-22z+q$ $-2z^3+8z^2-10z$ $3z^2-12z+q$ $3z^2-12z+15$ $q-15$	
			$\bullet^6$ state value of q [1,2]	$\bullet^6$ $q=15$	
			$\bullet^7$ obtain remaining two roots	$\bullet^7$ $1\pm\sqrt{2}\,i$	

Notes:
1. For candidates who substitute either $2+i$ or $2-i$ into the equation, obtain a correct value of q but who do not exhibit any other working, only $\bullet^6$ may be awarded.
2. $\bullet^6$ not available for a non-integer value of q.

Question			Generic scheme	Illustrative scheme	Max mark
17.	(c)		$\bullet^8$ show all four solutions on an Argand diagram [1,2,3,4]	$\bullet^8$	1

Question	Generic scheme	Illustrative scheme	Max mark

Notes:

1. Do not penalise the omission of the labels on the axes.
2. $\bullet^8$ is available only where 4 roots are illustrated.
3. Positional information is required for $\bullet^8$. In the illustrative scheme this is provided by the relative positions of the points. Where points are plotted inaccurately, positional information may be provided by coordinates e.g. (2,1) or the numbers 2 and 1 indicated on the appropriate axes. Accept $(2, i)$. The label $2 + i$ is not of itself sufficient to award $\bullet^8$.

Award $\bullet^8$
Points not in correct position relative to one another but coordinates given.

Do not award $\bullet^8$
Points not in correct position relative to one another and no coordinates given.

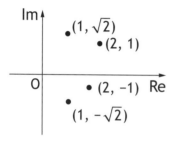

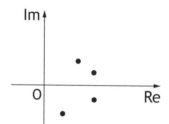

Do not award $\bullet^8$
Points not in correct position relative to one another and no coordinates given.

4. Accept separate labelled Argand diagrams.

Question	Generic scheme	Illustrative scheme	Max mark
18. (a)	•[1] evidence of use of product rule to find either $\frac{dx}{dt}$ or $\frac{dy}{dt}$ with one term correct	•[1] e.g. $\frac{dx}{dt} = \cos t + \ldots$	5
	•[2] obtain $\frac{dx}{dt}$ or $\frac{dy}{dt}$	•[2] $\frac{dx}{dt} = \cos t - t\sin t$	
	•[3] obtain remaining derivative	•[3] $\frac{dy}{dt} = \sin t + t\cos t$	
	•[4] state formula for instantaneous speed	•[4] $\text{speed} = \sqrt{\left(\frac{dx}{dt}\right)^2 + \left(\frac{dy}{dt}\right)^2}$ stated or implied at •[5]	
	•[5] obtain expression[1,2]	•[5] $\sqrt{(\cos t - t\sin t)^2 + (\sin t + t\cos t)^2}$ $= \sqrt{1 + t^2}$	

Notes:
1. At •[5] the simplification to $\sqrt{1+t^2}$ is not required.
2. •[5] may only be awarded for substitution into an expression of the form $\sqrt{(\ldots)^2 + (\ldots)^2}$.

Question	Generic scheme	Illustrative scheme	Max mark
(b)	•[6] evidence of valid strategy to find value of t and obtain at least one non-zero solution[1]	•[6] $0 = t\sin t$ and e.g. $t = \pi$	2
	•[7] choose correct value for t and calculate speed[1,2]	•[7] $t = 3\pi$ speed $= \sqrt{1 + 9\pi^2}$	

Notes:
1. For candidates who obtain an expression for $\frac{dy}{dx}$ rather than instantaneous speed, •[6] and •[7] are still available.
2. At •[7] accept a decimal answer provided it is accurate to at least 3sf (9·48).

ADVANCED HIGHER MATHEMATICS
2018

Question	Generic scheme	Illustrative scheme	Max mark
1. (a)	•[1] start differentiation[1]	•[1] $\dfrac{1}{\sqrt{1-(3x)^2}} \times \ldots$	2
	•[2] apply chain rule and complete differentiation[2,3]	•[2] $\dfrac{3}{\sqrt{1-9x^2}}$	

Notes:

1. For •[1] do not accept $\dfrac{1}{\sqrt{1-3x^2}} \times \ldots$ unless subsequently corrected.

2. For •[2] accept e.g. $\dfrac{3}{\sqrt{1-(3x)^2}}$ or $\dfrac{1}{\sqrt{\dfrac{1}{9}-x^2}}$.

3. For candidates who interpret $\sin^{-1}3x$ as $(\sin 3x)^{-1}$, •[2] is available for $-(\sin 3x)^{-2} \times 3\cos 3x$.

Question	Generic scheme	Illustrative scheme	Max mark
(b)	•[3] evidence use of quotient rule with denominator and one term of numerator correct	•[3] $\dfrac{5(7x+1)e^{5x}\ldots}{(7x+1)^2}$ **OR** $\dfrac{\ldots-7e^{5x}}{(7x+1)^2}$	2
	•[4] complete differentiation	•[4] $\dfrac{5(7x+1)e^{5x}-7e^{5x}}{(7x+1)^2}$	
(c)	•[5] start to differentiate product with one term correct[1]	•[5] $\dfrac{dy}{dx}\cos x + \ldots$ **OR** $-y\sin x + \ldots$	4
	•[6] complete differentiation of product[1]	•[6] $\dfrac{dy}{dx}\cos x\ldots$ **OR** $-y\sin x$	
	•[7] differentiate remaining terms	•[7] $+2y\dfrac{dy}{dx}=6$	
	•[8] express derivative explicitly in terms of x and y[2]	•[8] $\dfrac{dy}{dx}=\dfrac{6+y\sin x}{\cos x+2y}$	

Notes:

1. •[5] and •[6] are not available where the differentiation of $y\cos x$ leads to only one term.

2. •[8] is available only where $\dfrac{dy}{dx}$ appears more than once after completing differentiation.

Question			Generic scheme	Illustrative scheme	Max mark
2.			•[1] state expression	•[1] $\dfrac{3x-7}{x^2-2x-15}=\dfrac{A}{x+3}+\dfrac{B}{x-5}$	4
			•[2] form equation and find one unknown [1]	•[2] $3x-7=A(x-5)+B(x+3)$ **AND** e.g. $A=2$	
			•[3] find second unknown and write integral expression [1,2]	•[3] $B=1$ **AND** $\displaystyle\int\left(\dfrac{2}{x+3}+\dfrac{1}{x-5}\right)dx$ stated or implied by •[4]	
			•[4] integrate [3,4]	•[4] $2\ln\lvert x+3\rvert+\ln\lvert x-5\rvert+c$	

Notes:

1. •[2] and •[3] may be awarded where an attempt at factorisation leads to an incorrect linear denominator.
2. At •[3] disregard the omission of dx.
3. At •[4] disregard the omission of modulus signs.
4. •[4] is not available where the constant of integration has either been omitted or first appears after an incorrect logarithmic term.

Question			Generic scheme	Illustrative scheme	Max mark
3.	(a)		•[1] state general term [1,2]	•[1] $\dbinom{9}{r}(2x)^{9-r}\left(\dfrac{5}{x^2}\right)^{r}$	3
			•[2] simplify powers of x **OR** coefficients [1,2]	•[2] $2^{9-r}5^{r}$ **OR** x^{9-3r}	
			•[3] state simplified general term (complete simplification) [1,2,3]	•[3] $\dbinom{9}{r}2^{9-r}5^{r}x^{9-3r}$	

Notes:

1. Where candidates write out a full binomial expansion, •[1], •[2] and •[3] are not available unless the general term is identifiable in (b).

2. Candidates who write down $\dbinom{9}{r}2^{9-r}5^{r}x^{9-3r}$ with no working receive full marks.

3. •[3] is unavailable to candidates who in (a) produce further incorrect simplification subsequent to a correct answer eg $2^{9-r}5^{r}$ becomes 10^9 or x^{9-3r} becomes x^{6r}.

Question			Generic scheme	Illustrative scheme	Max mark
	(b)		•[4] determine value of r [1]	•[4] $r=3$	2
			•[5] evaluate term [1,2]	•[5] 672000	

Notes:

1. Where candidates write out a full expansion •[4] may be awarded where this is complete and correct at least as far as the required term. •[5] may be awarded only where the required term is clearly identified from the expansion.
2. •[5] is not available to candidates who interpret the term independent of x as substituting $x=0$.

Question			Generic scheme	Illustrative scheme	Max mark
4.	(a)		•[1] state conjugate	•[1] $\overline{z}_2 = p + 6i$ stated or implied	2
			•[2] substitute for z_1, $\overline{z}_2$, expand and apply $i^2 = -1$ [1,2]	•[2] $(2p - 18) + (3p + 12)i$	

Notes:

1. At •[2] accept $2p + 12i + 3pi - 18$.
2. To award •[2] $(2 + 3i)$ must be multiplied by another complex number.

	(b)		•[3] find value of p	•[3] -4	1
5.			•[1] start process	•[1] $306 = 2 \times 119 + 68$ $(119 = 1 \times 68 + 51)$	4
			•[2] obtain remainder of 17 [1]	•[2] $68 = 1 \times 51 + 17$ $(51 = 3 \times 17)$	
			•[3] express gcd in terms of 306 and 119	•[3] $17 = -1 \times 119 + 2(306 - 2 \times 119)$	
			•[4] obtain a and b [2,3]	•[4] $a = 2$, $b = -5$	

Notes:

1. At •[2] the gcd and the final line of working do not have to be stated explicitly.
2. The minimum requirement for •[4] is $306 \times 2 + 119 \times (-5) = 17$.
3. Do not accept $306 \times 2 - 119 \times 5 = 17$ where the values of a and b have not been explicitly stated.

6.			•[1] find $\dfrac{dy}{dt}$	•[1] $\dfrac{dy}{dt} = \dfrac{3}{3t + 2}$	5
			•[2] complete differentiation and relate derivatives [1,2]	•[2] $\dfrac{dx}{dt} = 2t$ and $\dfrac{dy}{dx} = \dfrac{\frac{dy}{dt}}{\frac{dx}{dt}}$ stated or implied at •[3]	
			•[3] evaluate gradient [2]	•[3] $\dfrac{dy}{dx} = -\dfrac{9}{2}$	
			•[4] find coordinates	•[4] $x = \dfrac{10}{9}$, $y = 0$	
			•[5] state equation of tangent [3]	•[5] $y = -\dfrac{9}{2}x + 5$	

Question	Generic scheme	Illustrative scheme	Max mark
Notes:			

Notes:

1. Evidence for $\bullet^2$ could include e.g. $\dfrac{dy}{dx} = \dfrac{\frac{3}{3t+2}}{2t}$.

2. Where candidates evaluate $\dfrac{dx}{dt}$ and $\dfrac{dy}{dt}$ before finding $\dfrac{dy}{dx}$, award $\bullet^2$ for evaluating the individual derivatives and award $\bullet^3$ for evaluating $\dfrac{dy}{dx}$.

3. At $\bullet^5$ accept eg $y + \dfrac{9}{2}x - 5 = 0$, $2y + 9x = 10$. Do not accept $y - 0 = \ldots$ or $y = -\dfrac{9}{2}\left(x - \dfrac{10}{9}\right)$.

Question	Generic scheme	Illustrative scheme	Max mark
7. (a)	$\bullet^1$ state transpose of C	$\bullet^1$ $\begin{pmatrix} -2 & 1 & 1 \\ 1 & -1 & 0 \\ 2 & 0 & -1 \end{pmatrix}$ stated or implied by $\bullet^2$	2
	$\bullet^2$ obtain matrix	$\bullet^2$ $2C' - D = \begin{pmatrix} -5 & 1 & 0 \\ -k-1 & -2 & -2 \\ 3 & -1 & -3 \end{pmatrix}$	
(b) (i)	$\bullet^3$ begin to find determinant	$\bullet^3$ $-(k+3)\begin{vmatrix} 1 & 2 \\ 1 & 1 \end{vmatrix} + 0\begin{vmatrix} 1 & 2 \\ 1 & 1 \end{vmatrix} - 2\begin{vmatrix} 1 & 1 \\ 1 & 1 \end{vmatrix}$	2
	$\bullet^4$ simplify expression	$\bullet^4$ $k+3$	
(ii)	$\bullet^5$ state value of k	$\bullet^5$ -3	1
8.	$\bullet^1$ differentiate	$\bullet^1$ $\dfrac{du}{d\theta} = \cos\theta$	4
	$\bullet^2$ find limits for u^3	$\bullet^2$ $u = \dfrac{1}{2}$, $u = 1$	
	$\bullet^3$ rewrite integral [1,2]	$\bullet^3$ $2\displaystyle\int_{1/2}^{1} u^4\,du$	
	$\bullet^4$ integrate and evaluate [4,5,6,7]	$\bullet^4$ $\dfrac{2}{5}\left[u^5\right]_{1/2}^{1}$ and $\dfrac{31}{80}$ (or $0\cdot3875$)	

Notes:

1. $\bullet^3$ is available where candidates either omit limits or retain limits for θ.

2. Where candidates attempt to integrate an expression containing both u and θ, where θ is either inside the integrand or erroneously taken outside as a constant, only $\bullet^1$ and $\bullet^2$ may be available.

3. Where candidates do not change limits but who produce working leading to $\dfrac{2}{5}\left[\sin^5\theta\right]_{\frac{\pi}{6}}^{\frac{\pi}{2}}$, $\bullet^2$ may be awarded.

4. For candidates who arrive at $\dfrac{2}{5}\left[\sin^5\theta\right]_{\frac{\pi}{6}}^{\frac{\pi}{2}}$ by inspection full marks are still available.

5. For candidates who integrate incorrectly, $\bullet^4$ may be available provided division by zero does not occur.

6. $\bullet^4$ is not available to candidates who write limits using degrees.

7. At $\bullet^4$ accept decimal answers rounded to at least 3 significant figures.

Question			Generic scheme	Illustrative scheme	Max mark
9.	(a)		•[1] form the sum of three consecutive integers [1,2,3,4,5] •[2] communication [1,5]	•[1] $(n-1)+n+(n+1)$ •[2] $3n$ which is divisible by 3	2

Notes:

1. Candidates may form the sum $n+(n+1)+(n+2)$ leading to $3(n+1)$ at •[2].
2. Withhold •[1] where candidates construct an expression of the form $an+(an+1)+(an+2)$, where $a \neq \pm 1$ and $a \in \mathbb{Z}$. •[2] may be available.

   eg $4n+(4n+1)+(4n+2)$ leading to $3(4n+1)$ which is divisible by 3.
3. At •[1] accept an expression such as $n+n+1+n+2$.
4. Withhold •[1] and •[2] where candidates form one (or more) sum of 3 specific consecutive numbers eg $2+3+4$.

| | (b) | | •[3] appropriate form for odd number, decomposed into two consecutive integers [1,2,3] | •[3] $2k+1=k+(k+1)$, $k \in \mathbb{Z}$ | 1 |

Notes:

1. Where candidates write down $2k+1=k+(k+1)$ and omit $k \in \mathbb{Z}$, award •[3].
2. Where candidates omit brackets and write down $k+k+1$ do not award •[3] unless the candidate demonstrates that k and $k+1$ are two consecutive integers e.g. writing $k, k+1$.
3. Where candidates begin with consecutive integers, •[3] may be awarded only where $2k+1$ is associated with any odd integer and not by a restatement of the assertion in the question.

| 10. | | | •[1] substitute, collect real and imaginary parts and equate moduli

 •[2] process to obtain a linear equation in x and y

 •[3] sketch consistent with equation [1,2] | •[1] $\|x+iy\|=\|(x-2)+(y+2)i\|$

 •[2] eg $y=x-2$

 •[3] complete sketch 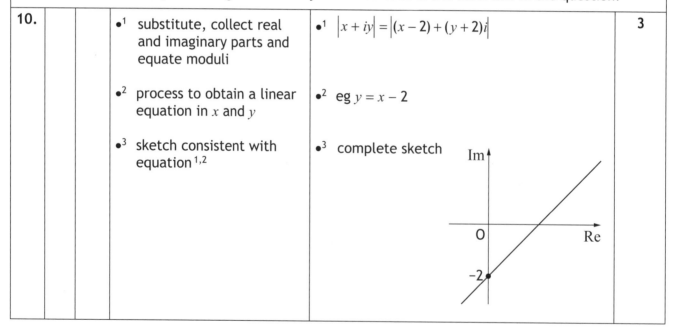 | 3 |

Question			Generic scheme	Illustrative scheme	Max mark
10.			**OR** •[1] interpret equation •[2] begin sketch of locus •[3] complete annotations[1,2]	**OR** •[1] line connecting (0, 0) and (2, −2) •[2] A straight line exhibiting any one of: bisection, perpendicularity, (0, −2) or (2, 0) •[3] A straight line exhibiting any two of: bisection, perpendicularity, (0, −2) or (2, 0) 	
			OR •[1] interpret separate loci[3] •[2] interpret conditions •[3] identify required locus[1,2]	**OR** •[1] two circles, centres (0, 0) and (2, −2) •[2] circles are congruent and intersect •[3] common chord extended beyond intersection points 	

Notes:

1. At •[3] accept any line passing through an appropriate point, which has positive gradient.
2. Do not withhold •[3] for axes which are unlabelled. Accept x and y in lieu of 'Re' and 'Im'. Disregard any appearance of i in the diagram.

Question			Generic scheme	Illustrative scheme	Max mark
11.	(a)		•[1] obtain A[1]	•[1] $\begin{pmatrix} \cos\dfrac{\pi}{3} & -\sin\dfrac{\pi}{3} \\ \sin\dfrac{\pi}{3} & \cos\dfrac{\pi}{3} \end{pmatrix}$	1

Notes:

1. Accept $= \begin{pmatrix} \dfrac{1}{2} & -\dfrac{\sqrt{3}}{2} \\ \dfrac{\sqrt{3}}{2} & \dfrac{1}{2} \end{pmatrix}$.

Question			Generic scheme	Illustrative scheme	Max mark
11.	(b)		$\bullet^2$ obtain B	$\bullet^2 \begin{pmatrix} 1 & 0 \\ 0 & -1 \end{pmatrix}$	1
	(c)		$\bullet^3$ correct order for multiplication $(P = BA)$	$\bullet^3 \begin{pmatrix} 1 & 0 \\ 0 & -1 \end{pmatrix} \dfrac{1}{2} \begin{pmatrix} 1 & -\sqrt{3} \\ \sqrt{3} & 1 \end{pmatrix}$	2
			$\bullet^4$ multiplication completed and appearance of exact values [1,2]	$\bullet^4 \dfrac{1}{2} \begin{pmatrix} 1 & -\sqrt{3} \\ -\sqrt{3} & -1 \end{pmatrix}$	

Notes:

1. Common factor not required for $\bullet^4$.
2. $\bullet^4$ is unavailable to candidates who have incorrectly identified $B = \begin{pmatrix} 1 & 0 \\ 0 & 1 \end{pmatrix}$.

Question			Generic scheme	Illustrative scheme	Max mark
	(d)		$\bullet^5$ valid explanation [1,2,3,4]	$\bullet^5$ eg compare the elements of P with the general form of a rotation matrix	1

Notes:

1. $\bullet^5$ may be awarded where a candidate's explanation makes reference to the specific entries of the leading diagonal of P ("they should be equal but are not") or trailing diagonal ("one must be negative of the other but is not")
2. Withhold $\bullet^5$ for a statement such as 'Matrix P represents a reflection' unless the reflection is specified e.g. 'Matrix P is a reflection in the line $y = -\dfrac{1}{\sqrt{3}}x$'.
3. $\bullet^5$ may also be awarded where candidates investigate the images of at least two points, neither of which is O.
4. Candidates who respond with reference to the constituent transformations of P may be awarded $\bullet^5$ only where there is reference to both transformations and communication demonstrates understanding that an even number of reflections are required in order to produce a rotation.

Question			Generic scheme	Illustrative scheme	Max mark
12.			$\bullet^1$ show true for $n = 1$ [1]	$\bullet^1$ LHS: $3^0 = 1$ RHS: $\dfrac{1}{2}(3-1) = 1$ So true for $n = 1$	5
			$\bullet^2$ assume (statement) true for $n = k$ **AND** consider whether (statement) true for $n = k+1$ [2,7]	$\bullet^2$ Suitable statement **and** $\displaystyle\sum_{r=1}^{k} 3^{r-1} = \dfrac{1}{2}(3^k - 1)$ **AND** $\displaystyle\sum_{r=1}^{k+1} 3^{r-1} = \dots$	
			$\bullet^3$ correct statement for sum to $(k+1)$ terms using inductive hypothesis [3]	$\bullet^3 \dots = \dfrac{1}{2}(3^k - 1) + 3^{(k+1)-1}$	
			$\bullet^4$ combine terms in 3^k [4]	$\bullet^4 \dfrac{3}{2} \times 3^k - \dfrac{1}{2}$	
			$\bullet^5$ express sum explicitly in terms of $(k+1)$ **or** achieve stated aim/goal **AND** communicate [5,6,7]	$\bullet^5 \dfrac{1}{2}(3^{(k+1)} - 1)$ If true for $n = k$ then true for $n = k+1$. Also shown true for $n = 1$ therefore, by induction, true for all positive integers n.	

Question	Generic scheme	Illustrative scheme	Max mark

Notes:

1. "RHS = 1, LHS = 1" and/or "True for $n = 1$" are insufficient for the award of $\bullet^1$. A candidate must demonstrate evidence of substitution into both expressions.

2. For $\bullet^2$ acceptable phrases for $n = k$ contain:
   ➤ "If true for…"; "Suppose true for…"; "Assume true for…".

   For $\bullet^2$ *unacceptable* phrases for $n = k$ contain:
   ➤ "Consider $n = k$", "assume $n = k$" and "True for $n = k$".
   An acceptable phrase may appear at $\bullet^5$.

   For $\bullet^2$, in addition to an acceptable phrase containing $n = k$, accept:
   ➤ "Aim/goal: $\sum_{r=1}^{k+1} 3^{r-1} = \frac{1}{2}(3^{k+1} - 1)$".

   For $\bullet^2$ *unacceptable* phrases for $n = k + 1$ contain:
   ➤ "Consider true for $n = k + 1$", "true for $n = k + 1$" ;
   ➤ "$\sum_{r=1}^{k+1} 3^{r-1} = \frac{1}{2}(3^{k+1} - 1)$" (with no further working)

3. At $\bullet^3$ accept $\ldots = \frac{1}{2}(3^k - 1) + 3^k$ or $\ldots = \frac{1}{2}(3^k - 1) + 3^{k+1-1}$.

4. At $\bullet^4$ accept $\ldots = \frac{1}{2}(3 \times 3^k - 1)$.

5. $\bullet^5$ is unavailable to candidates who write down the correct expression without algebraic justification.

6. Full marks are available to candidates who state an aim/goal earlier in the proof and who subsequently achieve the stated aim/goal.

7. Following the required algebra and statement of the inductive hypothesis, the minimum acceptable response for $\bullet^5$ is "Then true for $n = k + 1$, but since true for $n = 1$, then true for all n" or equivalent.

Question	Generic scheme	Illustrative scheme	Max mark
13. (a)	$\bullet^1$ Determine the relationship between x and h [1]	$\bullet^1$ $x^2 + h^2 = 2500$ $h = \sqrt{2500 - x^2}$	1

Notes:

1. Refer to general marking principle (m).

Question	Generic scheme	Illustrative scheme	Max mark
(b)	$\bullet^2$ interpret rate of change of x	$\bullet^2$ $\dfrac{dx}{dt} = -0 \cdot 3$	5
	$\bullet^3$ find $\dfrac{dh}{dx}$	$\bullet^3$ $\dfrac{dh}{dx} = -2x \cdot \dfrac{1}{2}(2500 - x^2)^{-\frac{1}{2}}$	
	$\bullet^4$ form relationship [6]	$\bullet^4$ $\dfrac{dh}{dt} = \dfrac{dh}{dx} \cdot \dfrac{dx}{dt}$ stated or implied at $\bullet^5$	
	$\bullet^5$ multiply by $\dfrac{dx}{dt}$ [1,2,6]	$\bullet^5$ $\dfrac{dh}{dt} = \dfrac{0 \cdot 3x}{\sqrt{2500 - x^2}}$	
	$\bullet^6$ evaluate $\dfrac{dh}{dt}$ [3,4,5,6]	$\bullet^6$ $\dfrac{dh}{dt} = \dfrac{9}{40}\,\text{cm}\,\text{s}^{-1}$	

Question	Generic scheme	Illustrative scheme	Max mark

Notes:

1. At $\bullet^5$ candidates may evaluate the derivatives separately e.g. $\dfrac{dh}{dt} = -0 \cdot 75 \times (-0 \cdot 3)$.
2. At $\bullet^5$ simplification is not required.
3. At $\bullet^6$ units are required. Accept decimal equivalent ($0 \cdot 225$ cms^{-1}).
4. Where candidates produce an incorrect answer, accept a decimal rounded to at least 2 significant figures.
5. Award $\bullet^6$ only where a candidate's final answer for $\dfrac{dh}{dt}$ is opposite in sign to that of $\dfrac{dx}{dt}$.
6. For candidates who do not show evidence of related rates, $\bullet^4$, $\bullet^5$ and $\bullet^6$ are not available.

Question	Generic scheme	Illustrative scheme	Max mark
14. (a) (i)	$\bullet^1$ multiply first term by a power of the common ratio[1,2,4] $\bullet^2$ find term[3,4]	$\bullet^1$ $\quad 80\left(\dfrac{1}{3}\right)^{\cdots}$ $\bullet^2$ $\quad \dfrac{80}{729}$	2

Notes:

1. At $\bullet^1$ accept any integer index other than 0 or 1.
2. Where candidates elect to repeatedly multiply, the minimum acceptable response for $\bullet^1$ is $80 \times \dfrac{1}{3} \times \dfrac{1}{3} \cdots$.
3. At $\bullet^2$ accept $0 \cdot 11$.
4. Award full marks for a correct answer with no working.

Question	Generic scheme	Illustrative scheme	Max mark
(ii)	$\bullet^3$ substitute[1,2,3] $\bullet^4$ find sum to infinity[1,2,3]	$\bullet^3$ $\quad \dfrac{80}{1-\frac{1}{3}}$ $\bullet^4$ $\quad 120$	2

Notes:

1. A correct answer without working receives no credit.
2. $\bullet^3$ and $\bullet^4$ are available only where a formula has been used.
3. At $\bullet^3$ candidates may use either the formula for the sum to infinity or apply a limiting argument using the formula for the sum to n terms (of a geometric progression).

Question	Generic scheme	Illustrative scheme	Max mark
(b) (i)	$\bullet^5$ substitute $\bullet^6$ find common difference[1]	$\bullet^5$ eg $\dfrac{5}{2}(2 \times 80 + (5-1)d) = 240$ $\bullet^6$ -16	2

Notes:

1. For a correct answer without working award 0/2.

Question	Generic scheme	Illustrative scheme	Max mark
(ii)	$\bullet^7$ find simplified expression	$\bullet^7$ $96 - 16n$	1

Question	Generic scheme	Illustrative scheme	Max mark
14. (c)	[8] set up equation	[8] $\dfrac{n}{2}[160 + (n-1)(-16)] = 144$	3
	[9] obtain quadratic equation in general form [1]	[9] $16n^2 - 176n + 288 = 0$	
	[10] find values of n [2]	[10] $n = 2$, $n = 9$	

Notes:

1. At [9] '= 0' must appear.
2. At [10] candidates must obtain 2 positive integer solutions.

Question	Generic scheme	Illustrative scheme	Max mark
15. (a)	[1] start integration by parts [1,2,3,4,6]	[1] $-\dfrac{x}{3}\cos 3x - \ldots$	3
	[2] complete integration by parts [1,2,3,4,6]	[2] $\ldots \displaystyle\int -\dfrac{1}{3}\cos 3x\, dx$	
	[3] complete integration [1,2,3,4,5,6]	[3] $= -\dfrac{x}{3}\cos 3x + \dfrac{1}{9}\sin 3x + c$	

Notes:

1. When integrating, candidates who repeatedly multiply by 3 cannot be awarded [1] but [2] and [3] may still be available.

2. Candidates who communicate an intention to integrate $\sin 3x$ and differentiate x but who inadvertently produce the derivatives of both $\sin 3x$ and x cannot be awarded [1] but [2] and [3] are still available.

3. For candidates who choose $\sin 3x$ as the function to differentiate and x as the function to integrate, [1] is available only where this is processed correctly. [2] and [3] are not available.

4. An error in sign when differentiating or integrating a trigonometric function should not be treated as a repeated error.

5. Do not withhold [3] for the omission of the constant of integration.

6. The evidence for [1], [2] and [3] may appear in (b).

Question			Generic scheme	Illustrative scheme	Max mark
15.	(b)		•[4] identify integral form of integrating factor[1,2]	•[4] $e^{\int -\frac{2}{x}dx}$	7
			•[5] determine integrating factor[3,6]	•[5] $\dfrac{1}{x^2}$	
			•[6] begin solution	•[6] $\dfrac{d}{dx}\left(\dfrac{1}{x^2}y\right)=\dfrac{1}{x^2}\left(x^3\sin3x\right)$ stated or implied at •[7]	
			•[7] rewrite as integral equation	•[7] $\dfrac{1}{x^2}y=\int x\sin3x\,dx$	
			•[8] integrate[4,5,6]	•[8] $\dfrac{1}{x^2}y=-\dfrac{x}{3}\cos3x+\dfrac{1}{9}\sin3x+c$	
			•[9] evaluate constant[4,6,7,8]	•[9] $c=-\dfrac{\pi}{3}$	
			•[10] form particular solution[4,6,7,8]	•[10] $y=-\dfrac{x^3}{3}\cos3x+\dfrac{x^2}{9}\sin3x-\dfrac{\pi x^2}{3}$	

Notes:

1. Candidates who attempt to solve the equation using e.g. separation of variables or second order method receive 0/7.

2. Candidates who attempt to apply integration by parts to the entire differential equation receive 0/7.

3. At •[5] accept an unsimplified integrating factor e.g. $e^{-2\ln x}$.

4. For candidates who omit the constant of integration, •[8], •[9] and •[10] are not available.

5. •[8] is available only where a candidate integrates correctly based on their RHS at •[7].

6. Where candidates obtain an integrating factor which is a constant, •[5], •[9] and •[10] are not available.

7. For candidates who proceed from •[8] by multiplying through by x^2: award •[9] for multiplying through by x^2 and award •[10] for evaluating the constant of integration then stating the particular solution.

8. For candidates who proceed from •[8] by multiplying through by x^2 but who fail to multiply the constant of integration, •[9] and •[10] are not available.

Question	Generic scheme	Illustrative scheme	Max mark
16. (a)	$\bullet^1$ set up augmented matrix	$\bullet^1$ $\begin{bmatrix} 1 & -2 & 1 & -4 \\ 3 & -5 & -2 & 1 \\ -7 & 11 & a & -11 \end{bmatrix}$	4
	$\bullet^2$ obtain two zeros[1]	$\bullet^2$ $\begin{bmatrix} 1 & -2 & 1 & -4 \\ 0 & 1 & -5 & 13 \\ 0 & -3 & a+7 & -39 \end{bmatrix}$	
	$\bullet^3$ complete row operations[1,2]	$\bullet^3$ $\begin{bmatrix} 1 & -2 & 1 & -4 \\ 0 & 1 & -5 & 13 \\ 0 & 0 & a-8 & 0 \end{bmatrix}$	
	$\bullet^4$ obtain value for a [3]	$\bullet^4$ $a = 8$	

Notes:

1. Only Gaussian elimination (ie a systematic approach using EROs) is acceptable for the award of $\bullet^2$ and $\bullet^3$.
2. For $\bullet^3$ accept any equivalent form.
3. $\bullet^4$ is not available unless the candidate's augmented matrix exhibits redundancy.

(b)	$\bullet^5$ introduce parameter and substitute[1,2]	$\bullet^5$ $z = t, \ y - 5t = 13$	2
	$\bullet^6$ equation of line[1,3]	$\bullet^6$ $x = 22 + 9t, \ y = 13 + 5t, \ z = t$	

Notes:

1. $\bullet^5$ and $\bullet^6$ are not available for substituting in either a numerical value or any expression in terms of a.
2. $\bullet^5$ is not available where the candidate substitutes into a row containing two other variables.
3. For $\bullet^6$ accept symmetric or vector form.

(c)	$\bullet^7$ write down normals[1,4]	$\bullet^7$ $\begin{pmatrix} 1 \\ -2 \\ 1 \end{pmatrix}, \begin{pmatrix} -3 \\ 5 \\ 2 \end{pmatrix}$ stated or implied	3
	$\bullet^8$ start to find angle	$\bullet^8$ $\cos\theta = \dfrac{-11}{\sqrt{38}\sqrt{6}}$ **OR** $\cos\theta = \dfrac{11}{\sqrt{38}\sqrt{6}}$	
	$\bullet^9$ find acute angle[2,3,5]	$\bullet^9$ $0{\cdot}75$	

Question	Generic scheme	Illustrative scheme	Max mark

Notes:

1. At $\bullet^7$ accept the use of $\begin{pmatrix} -9 \\ 15 \\ 6 \end{pmatrix}$.

2. Accept an answer in degrees which rounds to $43°$.

3. $\bullet^9$ is not available for incorrect working subsequent to a correct answer e.g. $90° - 43°$.

4. At $\bullet^7$ accept e.g. $\pi_1 = \begin{pmatrix} 1 \\ -2 \\ 1 \end{pmatrix}$ or $\pi_4 = \begin{pmatrix} -3 \\ 5 \\ 2 \end{pmatrix}$ but not at $\bullet^{10}$.

5. For candidates who express an answer in degrees, the degree symbol must appear.

Question	Generic scheme	Illustrative scheme	Max mark
16. (d)	$\bullet^{10}$ explanation [1,2,3]	$\bullet^{10}$ Planes π_2 and π_4 are parallel because the normal of π_4 is a multiple of the normal of π_2.	1

Notes:

1. For the award of $\bullet^{10}$ a statement must compare normal vectors or coefficients of x, y and z.

Accept eg $\begin{pmatrix} \dots \\ \dots \\ \dots \end{pmatrix} = -3 \begin{pmatrix} \dots \\ \dots \\ \dots \end{pmatrix}$ or 'The normals are multiples of one another' as justification for

the planes being parallel.

2. Do not accept a plane equating to a vector e.g. $\pi_2 = \begin{pmatrix} -3 \\ 5 \\ 2 \end{pmatrix}$.

3. Withhold $\bullet^{10}$ from candidates who provide a correct description but who subsequently write eg $\pi_4 = -3\pi_2$ or make reference to "direction vectors".

Question	Generic scheme	Illustrative scheme	Max mark
17. (a)	**Method 1** $\bullet^1$ first derivative and two evaluations **OR** all three derivatives **OR** all four evaluations $\bullet^2$ obtain expression [1] **Method 2** $\bullet^1$ write down Maclaurin series for e^x $\bullet^2$ substitute [1]	**Method 1** $\bullet^1$ $\begin{array}{ll} f(x) = e^{2x} & f(0) = 1 \\ f'(x) = 2e^{2x} & f'(0) = 2 \\ f''(x) = 4e^{2x} & f''(0) = 4 \\ f'''(x) = 8e^{2x} & f'''(0) = 8 \end{array}$ $\bullet^2$ $f(x) = 1 + 2x + 2x^2 + \dfrac{4}{3}x^3 \dots$ **Method 2** $\bullet^1$ $e^x = 1 + x + \dfrac{x^2}{2!} + \dfrac{x^3}{3!} \dots$ $\bullet^2$ $f(x) = 1 + 2x + 2x^2 + \dfrac{4}{3}x^3 \dots$	2

Notes:

1. Simplification might not appear until (c)

Question			Generic scheme	Illustrative scheme	Max mark
17.	(b)	(i)	$\bullet^3$ find $g''(x)$	$\bullet^3$ $g''(x) = 2\sec x \sec x \tan x$	**3**
			$\bullet^4$ evidence of product rule [1,2]	$\bullet^4$ $g'''(x) = 2\sec^2 x(\ldots) + (\ldots)\tan x$	
			$\bullet^5$ complete proof [3,4]	$\bullet^5$ $g'''(x) = 2\sec^2 x(\sec^2 x) + (4\sec^2 x \tan x)\tan x$	

Notes:

1. Candidates can be awarded $\bullet^4$ only where the product or quotient rule is required to differentiate their expression for $g''(x)$.
2. At $\bullet^4$ there must be clear evidence of the product rule (or quotient rule).
3. $\bullet^5$ is not available to candidates who obtain an incorrect answer at $\bullet^3$.
4. $\bullet^5$ can be awarded only where the candidate completes the differentiation correctly and shows clearly that the result is equivalent to the expression asked for in the question.

		(ii)	$\bullet^6$ completes **ALL** evaluations	$\bullet^6$ $g(0) = 0$ $\\ g'(0) = 1 \\ g''(0) = 0 \\ g'''(0) = 2$	**2**
			$\bullet^7$ substitute [1]	$\bullet^7$ $g(x) = x + \dfrac{1}{3}x^3\ldots$	

Notes:

1. $\bullet^7$ is available only for powers of x with numerical coefficients.

	(c)		$\bullet^8$ multiply expressions [1]	$\bullet^8$ $(1 + 2x + 2x^2 + \ldots)\left(x + \dfrac{1}{3}x^3\ldots\right)$	**2**
			$\bullet^9$ multiply out and simplify [2]	$\bullet^9$ $x + 2x^2 + \dfrac{7}{3}x^3\ldots$	

Notes:

1. For candidates who proceed via differentiation $\bullet^8$ is available for obtaining all three derivatives correctly.
2. $\bullet^9$ is available only for powers of x with numerical coefficients.

	(d)		$\bullet^{10}$ write down terms	$\bullet^{10}$ $1 + 4x + 7x^2$	**1**